Foreword by

Bernie Marcus, co-founder, The Home Depot

RAINMAKER!

MAKING THE LEAP
FROM SALESPERSON TO
SALES *CATALYST*

Carlos Quintero

Nancy Sutherland

© Sales Effectiveness Incorporated

Printed in the United States of America

ISBN 978-0-9676255-4-6

Published by:
Sales Effectiveness Incorporated
570 W. Crossville Rd. Suite 103
Roswell, GA 30075

770-552-6612

www.saleseffectiveness.com

Praise for "RAINMAKER!"

"One of the few sales training books that does not talk in circles. An easy to understand book on the hidden drivers that make the composite of a truly successful top producer. No one is born as a natural in selling...it does not exist. Understanding that we all have comfort zones, and getting outside of them from time to time, gets the best results we want for ourselves and for our team. RAINMAKER! 'un-mumbles the mumbo jumbo' that many sales gurus espouse. This book is not flash from a one day change-your-selling-life-seminar...but a guide to read and reread in the continuum of constant improvement. If this book was written for golf...I would finally break 100!"

Allen M. Soden
President - Half Full Group

"RAINMAKER! is a hands-on recipe book that will help teach good sales people the "secret sauce" that will help them join the very top echelon of sales experts. Every company has a few sales "superstars" and we are always looking for ways to teach the behaviors of our top sales leaders to the rest of the team. Mentorship programs are often reserved for only high-potential members of an organization. Here is a book that can provide that same type of expert guidance and support to every member of a sales force. This is one read that will be in the hands of my entire team as soon as it is released!"

Dan Davidenko
Vice President of Sales
Pearlman Enterprise; GranQuartz LP and Pearl Abrasive LP

"A sensational read and exceptional book for all existing Rainmakers and those striving to be one! A relevant story that brings together practical sales scenarios along with a great tool set for professionals who strive to advance their sales leadership."

Scott Rosenzweig
Vice President Sales, National Accounts & International
ORS Nasco, Inc.

"A rapid and enjoyable read that is as energizing as it is educational. As an entrepreneurial CEO, I couldn't wait to finish the book so that I could pass it on to my sales staff. These cogently conveyed sales teachings will make me money."

Garold L. Markle
CEO, Energage, Inc.

"RAINMAKER! is a very easy quick read told in a fun storytelling style that helps a salesperson improve... the book frames skills and concepts that every salesperson should be aware of and practice as they strive to be at the top of their game."

Jeff Davis
Vice President - Pacificrest Mills

"RAINMAKER! is a powerful, fun read. Carlos and Nancy have really connected the key dots, making the often misunderstood selling process very straightforward and easy to execute. Breaking the sales process down into the 5 roles is brilliant. This book is a must read for all sales teams looking to take their selling skills to the next level."

Colin Jaffe
Sr. Vice President Sales Operations - Behr Process Corporation

"RAINMAKER! presents a solid profile of the core essentials for both salespeople and their coaches from both a conceptual and application point of view. I was particularly impressed by the coaching / mentoring dialog style depicted - tomorrow's future sales manager would do well by modeling the practices of Ryan's mentor and by bringing in peer coaches as highlighted here."

Douglas Barnes
Vice President, Senior Director Global Sales Training - UPS (retired)

"The 21st Century "must read" for sales people that strive to be top performers. RAINMAKER! provides a blueprint for the attitude, discipline, activities and roles required for sales excellence."

Eric G. Blumthal
CEO - count5

"Experience has shown that the best salespeople don't excel solely on their own. They seek out the advice of others in becoming successful. They are stewards of their own learning, accountable for their own success. RAINMAKER! reinforces the importance of taking ownership for our own learning, in a fun, well-written and easy to understand story that demonstrates how salespeople can become both a change agent and trusted advisor."

Bill Hamrick
Vice President – Snelling Staffing Services

"This book goes about outlining an effective approach that the 'TOTAL' sales professional needs to have in today's challenging business environment. No longer can sales professionals make do without being truly well rounded. Carlos and Nancy take a fun and entertaining approach to describing why it's important to understand the multiple hats that sales people need to recognize and be good at in order to truly be effective and survive in today's competitive business climate. Anyone striving to be a true "Rainmaker" for their organization would benefit from understanding and using the core selling practices outlined in this book."

Mark Caccavale
Director Sales Force Effectiveness,
Sherwin-Williams – Diversified Brands

"The uniqueness of this book is its powerful and practical content delivered in a manner that emphasizes the need for a self-driven no "excuses" mentality by the sales person. The success of the sales manager as a coach is amplified when accompanied by a salesperson that takes the initiative to learn continuously. This is a must read for the salesperson that wants to demonstrate leadership as they take control of their career and success."

Paul Terlemezian
President - iFive Alliances, LLC

"I found the path of the book to be easy to follow and always pushing me to turn the page and absorb more. The story of Ryan and Valerie's venture into identifying the five roles of the Rainmaker had me almost immediately identifying and visualizing myself in each of these roles. The magic in this book for me was the simplicity of defining each role and the realization that someone 'gets it.' Strength in all five of these roles is a rarity in a sales professional but this book allows me to focus on the strengths and weaknesses of my team and provide valuable insights into how one might focus on improvement. This book provides both the vision and tools to help me guide and motivate each sales rep up from the middle of the pack."

Bob Neidig
President - Quality Window & Door, Inc.

"Every sales professional will recognize themselves through the story of Ryan. RAINMAKER! is an absolute "must read" for anyone wanting to become a true change agent in the sales profession. This is a well written, easy-to-follow book that reminds us all that the "Rainmaker" is in all of us. This book really does a great job of defining the steps we can all take to find a mentor and collaborate with fellow peers to unlock the methods of becoming a true sales professional. Once you understand and start to wear the five hats described in this book, you will find the roadblocks to becoming a successful sales professional disappear. This brings to reality what keeps even the most talented sales professionals from reaching their full potential. Compelling and incisive, this will become the definitive guide on how to bring proven results to the sales community.

Bret Day
Director, National Training – Behr Process Corporation

"This book provides a clear message on how to network, listen, and collaborate to produce best-in-class sales performance. A transformative message for sales excellence."

Steve Jansen
President – Four Seasons Consulting

"RAINMAKER! removes the mystery behind what it takes to be at the top of the sales profession. Disciplined execution and a relentless commitment to continuous improvement are the hallmarks of superior sales people. Engagingly told in an easy-to-read story format, RAINMAKER! is packed with ideas and methods that salespeople can use and apply to sharpen their game and move to the top."

Jay Davisson
President - Sherwin-Williams Paint Stores Group

"Being a change agent is not easy. And yet, that is the role of the salesperson of the future – helping customers improve their businesses through the products and services they represent and the solutions they provide. RAINMAKER! does a superior job providing salespeople with the tools and mindset they need to be successful. All salespeople will benefit from this book."

Steve Crouch
President - Newton Crouch, Inc.

"RAINMAKER! creates an articulate and practical explanation of the components of personal sales effectiveness, as well as a clear understanding of how those components work in tandem. The book clarifies how we can effectively manage our efforts – from identifying opportunities to turning those opportunities into business to assuring that we deliver on commitments. The empowering real-life analogies are helpful in demonstrating the value of understanding what a salesperson does in order to do it consistently day to day."

Stephen R. Gross
HLB Gross Collins

"There is perhaps no more misunderstood occupation than that of the professional salesperson. While everyone has heard the trite jokes and characterizations, the reality is much more demanding and structured. Rainmaker! provides a guidebook and a toolkit for the experienced and novice salesperson alike to move from caricature to professional business person – in short, the Rainmaker.

The experienced and successful salesperson as well as the rookie can benefit from this easy to read little book. Perhaps more importantly it can serve as a terrific reference for the Sales Manager, as it shows how to guide, support, and improve the sales professionals entrusted to their leadership. The tools provided can also be used to verify the sales process is being utilized and allow the setting of expectations and measurements that clearly lead to success, rather than routine call reports. Carlos and Nancy, thank you for this useful tool."

Jim Knudsen
Vice President of Sales and Marketing - Kysor/Warren

Contents

Foreword

I love selling. And I enjoy watching good salespeople "work their magic." Every person has to sell – no matter what your profession or what business you are in. For many people, selling is instinctive while for others it is not. Learning the intricacies of selling can be very helpful and will certainly help you in your career; these keys to selling can be learned in RAINMAKER!

Somewhere in the middle of this book, Valerie says, "…the best salespeople are the ones who can really put themselves in their customers' shoes. How do they feel? What keeps them up at night? What makes them tick?"

Those are the kind of salespeople (we called them associates) that Arthur Blank and I looked for when we co-founded The Home Depot. Our philosophy of customer service was, "Whatever it takes." That meant we would do whatever it took to satisfy a customer, within all human reason. It was taking ownership of customer problem resolution. But it was more than just customer service, it was customer *cultivation*.

So, what is the difference between customer service and customer cultivation? Customer service is getting the customer what they are looking for, explaining its use and sending the customer out the door. Customer cultivation results in the customer going out the door not only with the product and the knowledge of how to use it, but also an understanding of why that product is the best for their particular use. It means providing customers with whatever else they might need to do

i

their job effectively, the self-confidence that their task will be successful, and the knowledge that someone is always available to help. A good salesperson implements all five of the core roles highlighted in this book during customer cultivation, and that is why they achieve the title of "Rainmakers."

In RAINMAKER! the five core roles of most top salespeople are identified and explained: Hunter, Consultant, Influencer, Educator and Facilitator. The best salespeople understand each of these roles; they bring many with them on sales calls and use others throughout the selling process. Over the years it became very apparent when people were selling to us who were the "average" salespeople and who were the Rainmakers. We generally chose to do business with the latter.

Carlos Quintero and Nancy Sutherland have written "the" book that executives and salespeople should read to lead and succeed at selling. Selling can always use more "Rainmakers."

Bernie Marcus, co-founder
The Home Depot

Acknowledgments

The authors would like to thank the following people whose influence and relationships with us have helped shape the messages in this book:

Alan Cohen for his business acumen that challenged us to stay grounded as we crafted the story line; *Mike Wien* for his superior counsel on having the right message for our intended audience; *Marty Mercer* for his inspiration on the power of story; *Bruce Hoelzen* for his extensive experience on sales negotiations; *Larry Brambrut* for his editorial precision and creative mind; *Shirley Sillan* for her encouragement and context as a superior executive coach; *Tracy Stallard* for her insights resulting from the thousands of people she has trained; *Scott Harward* for his ability to synthesize ideas into powerful nuggets; *Bob Chaet* for his exceptional talent as a 'connector;' *Mike Kicidis* for exemplifying the essentials of being a street-savvy sales pro; *Joe Corcoran* for being the finest example of a Rainmaker we know, and *Pam Sligar* for keeping us organized in the process.

Thank you all for helping us to create this book about making rain!

*"We are what we repeatedly do. Excellence, then,
is not an act, but a habit."*

Aristotle

Chapter 1

A Case of "Average"

Ryan Gray walked out of his sales manager's office with mixed emotions crowding his head. His quarterly performance review with his manager at Summers, Inc. had just revealed that Ryan was performing 'as expected' for the quarter. Again.

As expected, thought Ryan. The same result he had heard in his last quarterly review. And the one before that. For some people – for lots of people, actually – this result might have been something to celebrate. But for Ryan, who had always tried to be on the high end of achieving, 'as expected' was like getting a 'C' on his report card. Not terrible, certainly not failing, but not the 'A's' and 'B's' that he always strived for in school.

What am I doing wrong? Ryan pondered as he returned to his desk. He thought about how hard he worked – starting early in the morning and calling on many more customers than the other salespeople. He put in longer hours too, pressing hard until long after many other salespeople had called it a day.

Two years ago, Ryan realized that he wasn't going to get ahead using only his rapport-building skills. While he had always been told that relationships make the difference in sales, he believed that relationship selling could only take him so far. So he started reading consultative selling books – books that would help him become a better business-to-business salesperson.

And he felt that he was making progress. He was becoming diligent in asking customers key questions about their business. He was trying to listen more rather than always trying to sell.

So, why, in spite of all his efforts, was 'as expected' the result once again? He could see that this year was probably not going to bring him the large bonus that he craved. No extra recognition. And he and his wife Michelle would not be on the elite company trip to Hawaii with the other top sellers. Again.

In thinking about who might be on the trip, Ryan was even more puzzled. He could easily think of four people from around the country that would earn the highest awards for the company this year. Gary, in Atlanta, was always one of the top sellers – he had made the trip every year since Ryan joined the company. Carmen, in Chicago, had been a top producer for years as well. James, in Dallas, and Luis – who was on Ryan's current team – had been steadily climbing the charts and both were blowing away their quotas this year.

Why? thought Ryan. *What am I doing… or not doing?* He scowled as he looked at the sales books on his shelf. During his review, Ryan's manager didn't provide much constructive help. "You're not doing badly, but you need to bump it up," he said. "Make more calls throughout the week. The numbers will come if you see more customers."

Easy for him to say, thought Ryan. *He doesn't realize how hard it is to find new customers today and continue to meet the demands from existing customers. There just doesn't seem to be any way to make it all happen.*

Since it was already 5:30 p.m., Ryan decided to pack it up for the day. He knew he should probably stick around for another hour to see if he could make a few more phone calls and catch some people late in the day, but right now, he just didn't have the heart for it.

I know I'm a good salesperson, he thought glumly as he packed up his briefcase. *But something's got to change.*

That night at home, Ryan knew he was becoming 'testy' with Michelle. Finally she asked him, "Hey, what gives? You've been barking at me all evening."

Ryan hadn't wanted to tell Michelle what was going on – with his review and his unsettled feelings about work. He really just wanted to take a break from thinking about all the things on his mind. But obviously, his unhappiness was showing through; he had no choice but to share it with her.

Michelle listened quietly as Ryan poured out his thoughts. They had known each other since high school, dated through college, and married soon after. She knew him as well as he knew himself.

"Right now, on the job, I'm a 'C' student." said Ryan. "I don't want to be *average* – not now, after all the hard work I've put in." He looked at her and shifted uncomfortably.

"You're not average," she said. "I've known you for a long time, remember? If there's one thing I've always admired about you, it's your determination. It sounds to me like right now the determination is there, but you don't quite know what to be determined *for*. Sales seems like it's pretty hard to define and you're shooting plenty of arrows, but a lot of them aren't hitting the target. So maybe you need to change your mindset with some target lessons."

"Target lessons? What are you thinking?" asked Ryan.

"I was thinking… remember back in high school when you were struggling through honors trigonometry? I recall you thought you were going to get a 'D' in it."

"Yes, I remember… but what does that have to do with anything?"

"What grade did you actually get?" asked Michelle.

"I got an 'A,' but it was really tough."

"Yes, so how did you finally get that grade?"

"Well, I studied my tail off, and then I had that tutor."

"Right ... that's what I was thinking," said Michelle.

"What do you mean?" asked Ryan. "As far as I know, there are no tutors in my field!"

"Are you sure? Have you ever thought about it?"

Ryan paused. It wasn't like Michelle to come up with crazy ideas, but this sure seemed like one. A tutor? Really?

"Just think about it," said Michelle. "Aren't there people in your field who have really mastered what they do? Maybe one of them would be willing to share some of their formula for success. You don't have to call it a 'tutor;' think of it as a mentor. From what I know about human nature, people who are asked for help usually like to give it."

Ryan had to admit that Michelle's instincts were generally on track. As a high-school guidance counselor, she helped kids every day. And she loved her work. Could there be someone out there that could help him see how to 'shoot his arrows straight' and make it to the top sales level within the company?

Ryan agreed to think about it for the next few days. He had always considered himself an independent person – he'd gotten this far in his job on his own and he certainly wasn't used to asking for help. Part of why he had gone into sales in the first place was because he knew that this is one field where a person can be the master of their own destiny. Yet he had to confess to himself that right now he must be missing some key ideas. His results just didn't bear out the level of effort he was putting in.

That night, Ryan mulled things over. He didn't feel he could ask any of his team members for help – like him, most of them fell into the 'average' pool and they all had their own issues to deal with. His current manager was 'all business' and Ryan didn't get the feeling that he would willingly become his 'mentor.'

So that exhausted the short list. Now, who else had been in sales for a long time and might have figured out the secrets of being consistently successful? He went through the possibilities. Finally, a thought popped into his head. What about Valerie – the woman who had first hired him at Summers, Inc.?

Valerie was Ryan's hiring manager five years ago. Unfortunately, she was only in that position for a few months after Ryan began because she was promoted to director in a different region. Ryan felt like he learned more from her in those first few months than he had learned in the 4½ years since. She was such a dynamic and caring individual – in the days when she sold for the company, she broke every record and as manager, she was phenomenal. She went on several sales calls with him when he first began which helped him get a strong start. Neither of the other two managers he had reported to since then had come close to possessing Valerie's sales savvy and ability to coach.

Ryan thought he heard that Valerie recently retired from the company and had relocated back to the area.

Tomorrow he would see if he could find out where she was… and if she might be willing to spend some time with him.

The next day, Ryan didn't have to search far to find Valerie Monroe's contact information. She was still listed in the company directory, but when he tried her number, her voicemail message stated:

> *"Hello. You've reached the former voicemail of Valerie Monroe. I am no longer with Summers as I officially retired on June 8. If you reach this number and are a customer of Summers, please contact my associate, Dave Clarkson, who will gladly help you or refer you to someone who can help. I've had a wonderful career at Summers and I believe our products, services, and people surpass the competition. So, just because I'm no longer 'officially' part of the team, know that I am still a firm supporter of what's happening at Summers. As always, thank you for your business."*

Ryan chuckled out loud and thought, *Isn't that just like Valerie – selling even after she's left the company.* He'd have to find another way to reach her.

Ryan thought, maybe, just maybe, Valerie was still monitoring her email through the company email server – or getting them forwarded to her personal account. He decided to take a chance and sent her a note.

Valerie,

I hope you remember me – you hired me as a new salesperson five years ago at Summers. There is something I'd like to discuss with you. Please call me at your convenience at 678-555-1234.

Thanks much,
Ryan Gray

We'll see what happens, thought Ryan. If he didn't hear from her in the next couple of days, he'd go further to try to find her. Surprisingly, though, the phone call came right after he finished his last sales call of the day. Just as he thought, Valerie was still monitoring her Summers email.

"Ryan?" Valerie's voice stated when he answered his phone. "Did you really think I might forget you?"

"Well, I wasn't sure – it *has* been over four years!"

"If there's one thing you should know about me, it's that I never forget the people I hired. I always thought you'd be one of our best salespeople. So how are you?"

They spent a few minutes catching up – Ryan shared some recent news from his division and Valerie told him what she had been up to.

"I decided that after many years in sales and sales leadership roles, it was time for me to take a break," she stated. "But to tell you the truth, I'm a little antsy to get my hands into something. Retirement isn't all it's cracked up to be."

Ryan smiled. "It actually sounds like you might be interested in hearing what I wanted to talk to you about."

Ryan filled Valerie in on some of his frustrations. "I know we can't fully get into it on the phone, but here's the bottom line. I, too, thought that I would be one of Summers' best hires, and five years ago I figured that by now I'd be one of the top salespeople. I'm doing okay, mind you, but being 'in the middle of the pack' is just not where I want to be. I work harder than almost anyone and I've tried different techniques, but I'm still not reaching that top 10%. My wife and I made the company trip my first year as one of the top new salespeople, but I haven't qualified for the trip in the past four years. Plus, my bonus just isn't where I thought it would be at this point."

"Hmmm," said Valerie. "I know that's frustrating for you. How can I help?"

"Well, Michelle and I were talking the other night – exploring ideas – and she suggested I find a mentor to give me some help. I seem to be stuck 'in the middle' and I can't seem to get out. She thought, and I agree, that I need to develop some new ways of thinking about my job. That's where you come in."

"Oh?" Valerie laughed. "How so?"

"Well, you seem to have had the 'magic pill' when you were in sales with Summers. You're still considered one of the top salespeople that ever worked at the company – and it's been years since you've been selling directly. I want to see whether, by any chance, you'd be willing to spend some time with me – helping me to figure out how to pull myself out of 'average.'"

"Ah," said Valerie. "It sounds to me like you want to become a *Rainmaker*."

"If you work just for money, you'll never make it. But if you love what you are doing, and always put the customer first, success will be yours."

Ray Kroc

Chapter 2

A Change in Mindset

Rainmaker. Ryan looked up the word in the dictionary later that night. The first definition read,

"A medicine man who, by various rituals and incantations, seeks to cause rain."

He laughed. Probably not what she meant.

The next definition said,

"Someone with the exceptional ability to attract and retain customers, bring in business, and increase sales and profits."

Ryan thought, *Now we're getting somewhere,* and he recognized that this could be the word to describe what he was seeking to become – one of the consistent top producers for the company. And Valerie may be the one to help him get there.

At the end of their phone conversation, Valerie had agreed to think about Ryan's proposal and come up with some options. They decided to meet for lunch on Thursday.

All week, Ryan tried even harder to analyze what made some of his fellow salespeople at Summers stand out and regularly win sales awards in the company. He had gotten to know them at regional meetings and through some joint project work. There didn't seem to be any pattern to their success – Gary was quiet and studious while Carmen was outgoing – almost boisterous. You'd be hard pressed to find two people more unlike each other – at least on the surface. Yet both of them were habitually at the top of their game – obviously they had figured out their own 'magic pill.'

James, one of the newer salespeople, had come from a competitor just a year ago and was already making a big name for himself at Summers. Ryan didn't know him very well, but he seemed like an average, run-of-the-mill guy. What was his secret? Luis, the other 'superstar,' had joined the company at the same time as Ryan; in fact, they had been in some of the same classes at Summers when they first began. He knew Luis was good and Ryan considered himself on par with him, but for some reason, Luis was now outperforming him – and most of the other salespeople in the company as well.

Could it be less the salesperson, and more the territory? Ryan considered this as he had many times in the past few years. But that theory didn't seem to hold any keys either. Sure, there were bigger customers in some territories, but all in all, he didn't feel like anyone had a huge advantage – not enough to explain the difference, anyway.

Thursday couldn't arrive quickly enough. Ryan had a morning meeting with one of his best prospects – Conway Associates. He had been calling on Conway for about six months and he thought they were very close to giving him a large piece of business. As he had been doing recently, he prepared lots of questions before the meeting to help surface their problems. By the end of the meeting, Conway had agreed to begin using Summers for one piece of their business – on a trial basis.

Once again, 'good,' but not 'great,' thought Ryan as he walked into the park. The city park was where Valerie suggested they meet today. *It will be a nice change of pace,* she had said. *Since I'm retired now, I'll bring some sandwiches and there are some tables near the pond that aren't usually crowded mid-day.* As Conway's offices were not far from the park, Ryan agreed, and looked forward to something other than his usual fast-food lunch.

He found the tables Valerie mentioned and sat down. Within minutes, he spotted a familiar figure walking toward the park tables. He stood up to greet her.

"Valerie – it's so good to see you!"

"Likewise," smiled Valerie.

"I don't want this to sound wrong, but are you sure you're old enough to retire?" Ryan asked. Valerie seemed rested and relaxed.

"Well, I may not have mentioned that I started working in sales when I was 12," Valerie joked. "Actually, the years go by pretty fast. I turned 55 just weeks ago and I decided to take some time for myself. It won't surprise me at all, however, if I don't last out here too long!"

Valerie unpacked the lunch she had prepared – sliced chicken on homemade rolls, fresh fruit, and iced tea.

"Wow," said Ryan. "I think if you put your mind to it, you could win cooking awards just as you did in sales!"

"Thanks. I'm enjoying trying out some new things," smiled Valerie. "So, let's talk about what's really on your mind today. Did you think about my suggestion that you want to be a *Rainmaker*?"

"I did. I had certainly heard the term before but I wasn't too familiar with what it meant in my context. But what I do know is this – I want to make more money and be one of the top salespeople in the field; if that's a Rainmaker, that's what I want to be."

"Good," said Valerie. "But first I want to set some expectations. We all know that money *is* important, but there's much more to becoming a *Rainmaker* than making lots of money. Financial success happens as a result of *a change in your mindset* about your role as a salesperson."

Ryan thought about his conversation with Michelle when she first brought up the idea of a mentor. She had used the same words … *'a change in mindset.'*

"What do you mean exactly?" he asked.

"Becoming a Rainmaker requires you to think differently than you have in the past. It's a place that not many salespeople ever reach. You know how it goes – all sales forces operate in a bell-shaped curve, with a *few* low performers, a *lot* of average performers, and a *few* top performers – the *Rainmakers*. This curve is a given in most sales environments."

She continued. "What those people at the top of the curve do differently is see themselves not as salespeople, but as sales *catalysts*. What do you think of when I say the word *catalyst*?"

"Well, my only context for that word would be from my old days in chemistry class. I believe it means a stimulus that causes a chemical reaction."

"Yes – in terms of chemistry, that's exactly what a catalyst does. In sales, a catalyst can be thought of as someone who is 100% focused on being a *difference maker* or *change agent*. They incite change in many ways, but their motivation is less about money and more about always bringing value to the customers they serve.

"In fact, Ryan, right now, I'm trying to be a catalyst to change *your* mindset!"

"Hmmm… a catalyst… a *sales catalyst*. Will thinking of myself as a catalyst help me to become a Rainmaker?"

"It will. Thinking of yourself in this way is actually one of the most important things you can do. You know, a lot of people think top salespeople are *born*, not *made*, and while I believe there are people who are more cut out for the world of sales, I also think that a lot can be done to turn an *average* salesperson into a *superior* salesperson – a Rainmaker. Considering yourself to be a catalyst is the first step."

"I like the idea," said Ryan. "Think of myself less as a salesperson – more as a catalyst."

Pausing for a moment, Valerie said, "Tell you what. I know it's going to be difficult for you to get away during the week – and I know what unpredictable schedules salespeople often have. What do you say we meet for a few weeks – on Saturday mornings – and we'll take a look at some concrete ideas that should help you get on the road to becoming a Rainmaker."

"Seriously?" said Ryan. "Would you be willing to do that?"

"Yes," said Valerie. "Let's see. The weather is supposed to be beautiful this weekend. Are you up for meeting on the river walking trail at 8:00 a.m. on Saturday?"

"Everyone lives by selling something."

Robert Louis Stevenson

Chapter 3

RAINMAKER

Saturday at 7:30 a.m., Michelle and Ryan coaxed their black Labrador, Bailey, into the car. Michelle thought she'd take Bailey to the river at the same time as Ryan and Valerie were on their 'Rainmaker' walk.

"Sounds like a plan," Michelle had said when Ryan told her about meeting with Valerie and having weekly sessions. Michelle met Valerie years ago at a holiday party and she recalled her as someone that almost anyone could relate to. "Good choice," she said, when Ryan revealed his 'mentor.'

Arriving at the park, Michelle and Bailey headed straight toward the river. Ryan scoured the parking lot and spotted Valerie stretching near her car. "Good morning!" said Valerie. "I'll be ready in just a second."

"No problem," said Ryan, watching Michelle begin to throw sticks for Bailey.

"Ready?" asked Valerie. She and Ryan quickly fell into pace on the trail.

"To get started," said Valerie, "why don't you share with me a little about yourself as a salesperson – tell me about your selling style and where you see your strengths."

"Okay," said Ryan. "My selling style is generally centered around building relationships with my customers. When I first began in sales, I was more of a *transactional* seller. You know, stopping by and asking customers if there was anything they needed… that sort of thing. But it didn't take me too long to learn that I wouldn't get far with that approach. So I began doing some reading and I attended a workshop where I learned more about consultative selling – how to ask questions to help my customers solve their problems. I think I've definitely improved along those lines."

"Great," said Valerie. "Consultative selling is an important approach in the business-to-business world. It's less about selling our products and services and more about what we can bring customers to help them grow their business. I applaud you for taking that initiative."

"Thanks," said Ryan. "I've read some books and I'm trying to put their ideas into practice. Some of it must be working because I get more business than I did in my early days. But it's just not enough anymore. I think I should be selling twice what I am today. That's what Gary and Carmen are doing."

"I'm glad you brought them up," said Valerie. "How are Gary and Carmen? They were big producers even while I was in the ranks."

"They're doing great! Well, at least they're *selling* great," said Ryan. They seem to *always* bring in big deals and have consistently high results. And I was thinking to myself just yesterday about how different they are as individuals, yet how similar their sales results are."

"It's interesting, isn't it?" said Valerie. "So who else would you say are the top producers right now?"

"James Miller. He came from the competition about a year ago. He's really knocking the socks off in his territory."

"I know him," said Valerie. "We actually met at a conference a few years ago and I've talked to him at various industry functions over the years. Good guy."

"Yes, he seems like it. I haven't gotten to know him well. It's frustrating to me though, that he's surpassed me – by far – in the short time he's been at Summers."

"Anyone else?" asked Valerie.

"Yes, Luis Suarez. Do you know him? He hired on at the same time I did. That one is frustrating for me too, since he and I have the same experience level. We've gone through workshops together and while I like him, I don't see him as having anything that I haven't got!"

"I remember Luis. From what I recall, he moved into sales from Customer Service."

"Yes, I think so," said Ryan. He wondered to himself, *Could that be the difference?"*

"So are those the people you would say are the consistent top sellers right now?" Valerie asked.

"Yes, I'd say so. Obviously there are other people that excel from time to time, but these four seem to stand out all the time – that's where I want to be."

"Okay," said Valerie. They were nearing the top of a hill and the conversation paused while they caught their breath.

Finally Valerie spoke. "It's interesting that you told me the names you did today because I think they actually provide a great illustration for a 'model' that I'm going to introduce you to."

"A model? Tell me more."

"Early on when I was in sales, I set out to be a Rainmaker. I studied the people who were most successful to see if I could pinpoint some of their characteristics and traits so I could try to emulate them. As the years went on, I found that there seemed to be certain qualities that were 'part of the DNA' of the salespeople who continually excel. And while I say these things are part of their DNA, I don't mean that they were *born* with these characteristics and traits; they just seem to be part of how they function on a regular basis."

She continued. "I became so intrigued with these ideas that in my last few months at Summers, I spent time documenting my findings and even formed an ad hoc *Sales Excellence Council* within the company to help. Just before I left, we submitted a summary to the CEO but I really don't know if anything has happened with it."

"Now I'm really curious. What did you find?"

"After lots of study and research – not only with our own people, but other top salespeople as well – we came up with *five core roles* of most salespeople who become Rainmakers. We developed a 'model' of the five roles and called it the 'Catalyst' model. We labeled the five roles – or hats, if you will – that these people wear as:

- HUNTER
- CONSULTANT
- INFLUENCER
- EDUCATOR
- FACILITATOR

Valerie paused. "What's your first reaction to these five roles?"

Ryan said, "My reaction is that I want to learn more about your findings. I did hear the word Consultant in that list, and that's certainly what I've been striving to become to my customers, but maybe I've only been focusing on one out of five – or 20% – of the roles of Rainmakers. Scary thought."

"I would guess you're actually practicing all five of them to some extent. The difference is that Rainmakers focus more *deliberately* – more *purposefully* – than you have likely been doing. Remember our conversation about thinking of yourself as a catalyst? These people have figured out that practicing the five roles will lead them there. It sounds like you've begun making progress in wearing the *Consultant* hat, and that's terrific. Focusing on just one area by itself, however, will probably not make you a Rainmaker."

"Sounds like I have some work to do," said Ryan. The two made the last turn back toward the parking lot.

"It's an exciting time to be in sales," said Valerie. "Companies are viewing sales with even more significance than ever. And there are all kinds of innovative developments that can help us – things like social networking and new technologies we can put to use. I don't think most people have fully figured out how to blend the tried and true sales principles with the latest and greatest technologies. I'm trying to keep fresh on all of it – that's the *catalyst* in me."

Whew, thought Ryan. *No wonder Valerie was so successful – even after retirement she continued to press on, learning and doing more than most salespeople do mid-way through their career.*

"I can't believe we've covered three miles already," said Ryan. "I'm really grateful to have this opportunity to learn from you. I hope that you're willing to keep working with me for a while!"

"I'm looking forward to it. And if the research around these roles and traits resounds well with you, I plan to take on some consulting work – after I've had a short sabbatical!"

"Well, I'm happy to be your guinea pig. So next week, same time, same place?"

"Actually, if you don't mind, next week I'd prefer if you come over to the new office I'm renting. My husband already had a home office and I needed some space of my own. It's not far from the Summers building. Will that work for you?"

"Sounds great."

Just then, Ryan spotted Michelle and Bailey jogging up from the river. Michelle and Valerie greeted each other warmly and Valerie played with Bailey for a few minutes. Watching them, Ryan allowed himself a quick thought. *Maybe I really can break out of average this time.*

*"Unless you try to do something beyond
what you have already mastered, you
will never grow."*

Robert Osborne

Chapter 4

The Five Roles

All week, Ryan thought about his conversation with Valerie. *Five roles of a Rainmaker*, she had said. *Act as a 'catalyst' of change.* Prior to this, Ryan considered himself one of the more astute salespeople at Summers. He certainly felt he put more effort in than many others. Had he really missed the boat? He was determined not to let his frustration get to him. *Remember what happened during that Trig class*, Michelle reminded him. *You felt overwhelmed at first then too.*

Driving to Valerie's office the following Saturday, Ryan wondered how she would teach him about the five roles of a Rainmaker. What were the roles again? He remembered the first two – *Hunter* and *Consultant*. He knew that he had been working at becoming more like a *Consultant* and he had certainly heard the term *Hunter* used in the world of sales, but he couldn't recall the other roles. He wondered how Valerie had come up with them.

She looked up when he arrived. "Welcome," she said, "This place isn't too big, but it serves my purposes very well. Would you like some coffee?"

Ryan looked around as Valerie poured the coffee. Her office had a very calming feel and she had brought in several wood carvings and other unusual artwork. He thought it suited her perfectly. He commented on it as she handed him a coffee mug.

"Thanks. We've been able to do a lot of traveling over the years and my husband and I often try to buy unusual artifacts when we're in a new place."

She invited Ryan to sit down and then said, "Since last week, I created a few slides that I thought might help. Take a look."

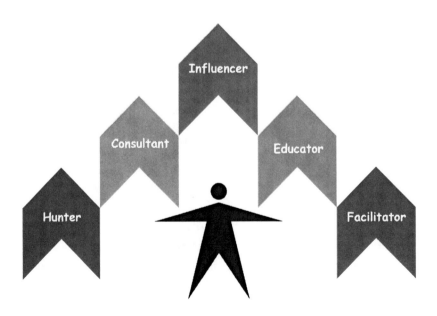

"As I mentioned, Rainmakers wear five hats:

- HUNTER
- CONSULTANT
- INFLUENCER
- EDUCATOR
- FACILITATOR

Ryan studied the slide. "I just noticed something," he said. "If you reverse the first two, there's an acronym that might help me to remember the roles."

Valerie laughed, "You're right; it *would* spell 'CHIEF,' wouldn't it? Even though there's a reason we listed the roles in the order we did, thinking of them using the acronym 'CHIEF' may help people recall the roles. Nice insight!"

"Thanks," laughed Ryan. "So do you mean that top salespeople wear all of these hats all the time?"

"No, not all at *one* time. It might be easier to think of the roles as a sort of 'continuum.' At one end, when a salesperson is focused on being a *Hunter*, they are relentlessly pursuing new business; at the other end, as a *Facilitator*, they are ensuring that customers are completely satisfied and that they and the company deliver on all commitments made. In between, the Rainmaker is a vital *Consultant*, a powerful *Influencer* and an expert *Educator*. Thinking of the roles in this way, you realize that Rainmakers have the ability to focus on the area that is most required at the time."

She continued. "While the best Rainmakers practice all five roles at various times as needed, some people are more skilled and more naturally adept in one or more areas - and there's nothing wrong with leveraging these natural abilities.

"You, for example, are drawn to the *Consultant* role – and I believe it can serve you well. You enjoy solving customers' problems and offering ideas to help them grow their business. I, on the other hand, started out as more of a *Facilitator* – I relished the challenges of overseeing product implementations and making sure all my customers' requirements were met. I still love that part of sales – there's nothing that gives me more satisfaction than having a customer write a letter of thanks that we exceeded their expectations."

Ryan thought back to the message he had heard on Valerie's voicemail. He could understand why customers were so blown away by her dedication and commitment.

"Soon enough though," said Valerie, "I found that focusing only on facilitating and supporting my customers was not going to make me a Rainmaker. Good facilitation is one of the most important aspects of sales in my opinion – and one that is often overlooked by many salespeople – but I knew I needed to do more to get to that upper echelon."

"So is that when you started studying the habits of other successful salespeople?" Ryan asked.

"Yes. I made a conscious decision to watch them… talk to them…see what stood out in how they brought in and retained business. It's my guess that if you studied the people we talked about last week, you would see the five roles in each of them. Like you and I, they probably have one or two roles they are more naturally drawn to, but my guess is they've honed their skills in each area."

"Sounds like I need to branch out a bit."

"You're a good salesperson, Ryan. To reach the level of Rainmaker, though, it takes getting out of your comfort zone sometimes."

"Well, I know I want to be at the top and I'm ready to get started. Where should we begin?"

"Before we get started, I'd like to bring up a potentially sensitive topic. One thing that concerns me just a bit is that I've heard you say a number of times that you want to be at the top of the list… make the trip… get a bigger bonus, etc. And I understand that; I really do. But have you ever heard of the term 'intrinsic motivators?'"

"I don't think so."

"Researchers have spent a lot of time trying to find out what makes people more successful in many fields – sales being one of them. They found that the most successful people are those who are more motivated by what are known as 'intrinsic' factors – like helping their customers succeed and grow – than 'extrinsic' factors like making more money or the power and prestige that go along with that."

She continued. "Let me ask you, what does your wife do?"

"She's a high school counselor."

"Terrific! And is she successful in her field?"

"Very. She's the first one that most students and administrators turn to when they need help."

"Would you say that money is her primary motivation?"

Ryan laughed. "Are you kidding? I don't think that's the primary motivation for anyone in that arena. No, she's definitely motivated by helping her students through their problems and helping them to succeed at the next level."

"Isn't it interesting? In her world, that's what defines success. Somehow, we've got to grab on to that idea in the world of sales – instead, so many salespeople are motivated primarily for their own benefits. They're so focused on making more money or getting glory for themselves that they have forgotten a few of the core principles of sales – customers buy from people they *like, know* and *trust.* They want to work with people who bring real value to them and their companies; people who care about them and want to help them reach their personal and professional goals."

Valerie continued. "In sales, we're very fortunate because we can earn rich financial rewards from living by those core principles." She paused. "Unfortunately, I've found there are an awful lot of salespeople out there that are more focused on their own success than their customers' success."

"Hmmm...," said Ryan. "I think you're saying that I may be a little too tied up in thinking about Hawaii right now?"

"Maybe. I know you're a good salesperson, Ryan. You're optimistic and have a natural rapport with people and those strengths will serve you very well. Still, you may need to work on developing your intrinsic motivators a bit further."

She continued. "None of this is to say that I'm all about a 'soft' approach in selling – believe me, I can be as competitive as they come and I'm driven to achieve the highest goals. But at the heart of my work is *always* my ultimate purpose – to help my customers succeed. We'll talk more about that as we go."

Ryan listened intently and Valerie paused to let her message sink in. This idea, she knew, was a 'paradigm shift' for many people in sales who have always been taught that closing the deal was their primary purpose.

After a moment, Valerie said, "I'm sharing this with you now because I don't want you to go into our work together with the idea that being a Rainmaker is only about the financial rewards. It's really *bigger* than that and I want you to expand your mind as we get started on this journey together."

She pulled up another slide and let Ryan read through the bullet points.

In Sales, a *Rainmaker* is someone who:

- Brings in BIG business. Is a steady producer who finds a way to make budget / goals /targets year after year.
- Provides superior value that *draws* more business to them.
- Focuses intently on being a top performer – an eternal optimist.
- Is motivated by the intrinsic benefits of being a change agent, making a difference and creating value for customers.
- Adapts a mindset of continuous improvement and learning.

After a few moments, Valerie asked, "Are you starting to see where I'm going with this? Rainmakers are more than the men and women at the top of the sales lists. They are the people that make things happen. They are the difference makers. *They bring about change.* They're not just 'going through the motions' in their interactions with customers. These people maintain a frame of mind that I believe you can adopt."

"To tell you the truth, I'm a little overwhelmed with all these ideas right now," said Ryan. It's a lot to absorb."

"I agree. It is a lot to absorb at one time. That's why I think a good approach would be to take a week or two to talk about each of the roles – including what the research shows about them and some of the best practices that align with each role. Then I'll provide you with some 'tools' that will help you explore each of the roles and put them into practice."

"Tools?" asked Ryan.

"Yes. During my career, I created and collected various tools used by some of the best salespeople I knew. I introduced some of these ideas to my own sales teams along the way. I believe you'll find that the practices and the tools will help you in your journey of becoming a Rainmaker. I think of them as my 'secret sauce.'"

"Well, I was really hoping for a 'magic pill' but I guess a 'secret sauce' will work just as well!" laughed Ryan.

Valerie smiled. "Yes, I know that many salespeople think that Rainmakers have some sort of 'magic pill.' Why else would they have consistently higher results than others who work just as hard? The truth is that there is no magic pill as such. However, there *is* magic that can occur if you consciously and deliberately pursue the ideas we're going to explore over the next few weeks.

"The beauty of all this is that this magic is achieved not necessarily by working *harder*. The best salespeople have learned how to work *smarter* and the skills and strategies we'll be discussing will help you with that."

"That's great," said Ryan. "When do you want to begin?"

"Let's take a week off to let me put some of my ideas into a more organized structure. Meanwhile, maybe you can spend some time doing some of your own 'field research' by really studying some of the practices and traits of the best salespeople you know. We'll get back together in two weeks, okay?"

"Sounds good. I've certainly tried to observe what others are doing and I've talked to many people over the years, but I wouldn't say I've really 'studied' them. I'll do it. Until then, I look forward to our next meeting."

"Don't join an easy crowd. You won't grow. Go where the expectations and the demands to perform are high."

Jim Rohn

Chapter 5

Evolution of a Salesperson

Driving home from Valerie's office that day, Ryan felt more optimistic about his future than he had in a long time. It seemed like he was finally being let in on the 'secrets' known by the best salespeople. He knew they weren't really secrets, but on the other hand, they certainly weren't obvious to him.

Over the several days, he took Valerie's advice and started paying closer attention to some of the salespeople on his team – especially the most successful ones. That included Luis – one of the *Rainmakers* he and Valerie had spoken about earlier. Luis, he knew, had worked at call centers, first with a competitor and then with Summers, before moving into sales.

It was apparent that his customers thought very highly of Luis – no one else on the team had been able to retain and grow their customer base as well as he had. After their weekly team meeting on Thursday, Ryan decided to take a direct approach and walked over to him.

"Luis, can I buy you a cup of coffee?"

"Sure. What's up?"

They walked towards a table in the cafeteria. "We've known each other for a while now and obviously, based on your results, you're doing a lot of things right. I'd like to compliment you on all the success you've achieved recently."

"Thanks – I'm flattered!" laughed Luis as they sat down.

Ryan continued. "I have a favor to ask. I'm a little frustrated with my results and I'm really working on improving my game. I wanted to see if you might be able to give me any words of advice on how you continue to surpass your goals. And by the way, please know that I'll be happy to help you in any way I can as well – whether now or on a future project!"

Luis sipped his coffee and smiled. "I might take you up on that someday! Actually, I'm happy to help if I can."

Luis continued. "Let's see – what am I doing to surpass my goals? One area I've really been focusing on lately is going after bigger deals – the 'elephants,' if you will. You may know that my largest customer has been The Corley Company – I've had a very successful run there. Last year I decided to put 90% of my effort into going after companies like them. So I did a lot of research on businesses with similar characteristics and I've been heavily targeting a few of them."

He continued. "So I'd say the first approach I'm using is to go after companies with *large* opportunities. Then, once I break in to one of these companies, I'm like a 'mole;' I just keep working through the layers until I've met people in most of the divisions. Finally, after a sale, I review and continually monitor the implementation plan – from top to bottom – to be completely certain that everything goes as planned. I don't want my customers to even *think* about going somewhere else because of a glitch. My strategy seems to have paid off – now instead of one big customer, I have three!"

Ryan thought about his customer base. He knew he had more customers in number than Luis did this year, yet Luis' overall revenues were considerably higher. Ryan was closing deals all the time, but he wouldn't call any of his customers *'elephants.'*

Note to self, thought Ryan. *Bag more elephants.*

"Thank you," said Ryan. "You made some great points. I know you've got a lot to do and so do I, but would you mind if I pick your brain every once in a while? I'd especially like to ask you more details about how you monitor the implementation plans."

"Not at all," said Luis. "Even though it's not actively promoted in our group, I strongly believe that we should all be supporting each other on the team. When *one* of us wins, we *all* win in my book."

Ryan thanked Luis again as they finished their coffee. Later he thought back to his first conversation with his wife. *Most people like to help when they are asked,* she said. Maybe his ego had been in the way before. This asking for help thing wasn't all bad…

In the next few days, Ryan did a bit more 'field research,' thinking about and studying some of the other Rainmakers in the company. Some ideas were starting to gel for him when he and Valerie got together again.

This week they decided to meet at Valerie's office again. After they sat down, Valerie began. "So, did you discover anything important in the past couple of weeks?"

"Yes. I discovered that there are a lot of good people out there – people who have plenty of ideas to offer someone who is willing to learn."

"Great! That in itself, you'll find, is one of the most valuable lessons learned by Rainmakers. They are constantly on a quest to learn more – I call it a path of *continuous improvement*' and that path never ends."

"Really? That could be a little discouraging," said Ryan. "It makes me feel like I've started too late."

"On the contrary. It's literally never too late. And Rainmakers truly relish learning – they read, they discuss, they take workshops, they practice. They enjoy where the ride takes them."

"It's funny you say that. I guess part of me wanted to think that I've been working in sales for five years now and I should already know what it takes to do the job well!" said Ryan.

"Ha! Five years is nothing! I was in sales for 25 years and I'm still learning today. Even now I find it fascinating when I discover a new way to reach a customer. That's what keeps the work so interesting!"

"I think I'm starting to 'get' that," said Ryan. He thought about how good it felt when he had tried a new approach and it actually paid off. He had just never focused on the idea of constant learning before.

"Let me show you something, while we're on this topic," said Valerie. She searched her files and found a slide.

"Since we're talking about continuous improvement, this graphic shows five stages – depicting what typically happens as salespeople evolve in their career.

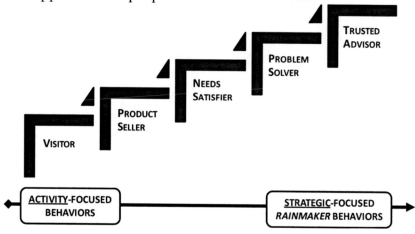

"Let's walk through these steps, shall we?" said Valerie.

VISITOR. When most people begin in sales, they're often a little nervous and intimidated by all they have to learn about the job and by calling on customers. So they 'drop in' for a quick 'visit.' They try to visit as many customers as they can and typically say things like, *'I just stopped by to see if there might be anything you need today.'* Their interactions with customers usually involve building rapport and promoting what's 'on special,' if you will.

PRODUCT SELLER. Next, as a salesperson learns more and gains more experience, they become more proficient in the 'nuts and bolts' of whatever they're selling. They place more focus on the features and benefits of their products and services. They know how their products work and they help customers see how the products and services can be used. They gain a bit more traction than 'visitors,' but sometimes salespeople get 'stuck' as product sellers.

NEEDS SATISFIER. As time goes on, most salespeople realize that uncovering more of what the customer *needs* provides them with greater success. They make it their practice to 'unearth' two or more needs and they position how their products and services can satisfy those specific needs the customers has expressed.

PROBLEM SOLVER. Good salespeople then try to get to the next level – the one called 'problem solver.' Most professional salespeople think they are there, but some really aren't – they've 'stalled out' at satisfying needs. Problem solvers are skilled at digging deeper to uncover a customer's true 'pain' and then determining what solution he or she can offer to relieve or alleviate that pain. They bring in others – either subject matter experts within the company or even outsiders – to help identify issues and offer solutions. A good problem solver typically has fewer customers, but the *size* of their sales is increasing. Rather than looking for only 'product or service fit,' the salesperson looks for a strong 'business fit' between the companies. They fully understand their customers' business and the industry. Sales are more complex and the sales cycle is longer.

TRUSTED ADVISOR. The best salespeople become trusted business advisors to their customers. This is a level that is never reached by many salespeople. These sales pros not only react to changes within the industry – they *anticipate* change and lead their customers through it because they fully understand the implications of what's occurring. They're sought out by customers for their opinion and advice. The primary focus at this level is around business issues and the *value* that the salesperson and their company can provide – a far cry from the price and frequency focus of the 'visitor' salesperson.

After they looked at the slide together, Valerie asked, "So, where do you think you currently fit?"

Ryan thought back to his earlier conversation with Luis and how he was 'targeting' specific companies to call on. Ryan knew his own strategy had generally been to call on as many customers as possible.

"In general, I'd say I'm probably somewhere between a Needs Satisfier and Problem Solver." He paused. "I like the visual. It helps me see the progress I've made...and where I want to go."

"I bet if we asked most top salespeople how they evolved," said Valerie, "their story would be similar; some faster, some slower, of course. Keep in mind that depending on the situation, you can fluctuate between the stages. For example, some customers need you to be more of a Needs Satisfier than Trusted Advisor at times."

She continued. "But Rainmakers tend to spend more time in the top two stages – Problem Solver and Trusted Advisor. Their customers often come to them, and they see themselves as *catalysts* to help change their customers' businesses for the better. They solve problems, identify opportunities, provide business advice, anticipate future needs, and in many cases, know as much about the business as the customer does."

"I can see that," said Ryan. "At first, the person is focused on *activities* and making frequent visits and at the higher levels, it's more *strategic*."

"Exactly," said Valerie.

Ryan then told Valerie more details about his conversation with Luis. "We're in the same department…with the same resources and the same manager… yet on his own, he's taking a very different, more strategic approach."

He ended by saying, "You know, it seemed a little awkward at first asking Luis for help, but it really opened my eyes to start thinking in a different way."

Valerie laughed. "That's another pet peeve of mine," she said. "Most salespeople are independent by nature and many have a pretty large ego – both of which can be good qualities in the world of sales. On the down side, it means we don't like to ask for help. One big lesson I've learned over the years is that asking for help is actually a sign of strength – not weakness, as many fear. It's a *smart* person who knows they can't learn everything on their own."

Ryan could tell this was a personal 'hot button' for Valerie. He had so much respect for her that it was a relief to know she didn't think less of him for asking for help. He laughed. *"Continuous learning,* right?"

"I like your attitude," smiled Valerie. "Okay, I'm sure you can tell that I have a lot of passion around that subject. Now let's move ahead. We'll start by looking at the first of the five Rainmaker roles I introduced you to earlier - *Hunter."*

"The quality of a person's life is in direct proportion to their commitment to excellence, regardless of their chosen field of endeavor. Leaders are made, they are not born. They are made by hard effort, which is the price which all of us must pay to achieve any goal that is worthwhile."

Vince Lombardi

Chapter 6

HUNTER

Valerie began. "So, Ryan, what comes to mind when you hear the word 'Hunter?'"

"I've heard the terms 'Hunter' and 'Farmer' throughout my career in sales," said Ryan. "A Hunter is someone who goes after new business while a Farmer is someone who takes care of – or 'farms' – existing customers."

"At a very high level," said Valerie, "that is how they've traditionally been defined. I've always liked the word 'Hunter' because I think it evokes a vivid image of someone who is really *going after* what they want. Have you ever thought about the word that way?"

"Honestly? No, I never gave it much thought. But I've always considered a Hunter and a Farmer to be at opposite ends of the spectrum – you're either one or the other."

"That's where we sometimes run into a problem," said Valerie. "The idea that all salespeople are either Hunters *or* Farmers always bothered me. I think it's oversimplifying what people are capable of. Often, Rainmakers are both strong Hunters *and* Farmers."

She continued. "Anyway, we chose to keep the word 'Hunter' as one of the five roles of a Rainmaker. Even though it's a well-used word in sales, it's still the right word to describe someone who is always seeking that next opportunity and who is able to see and sense where potential exists. To me, the word 'Farmer' is too simplistic for the many other activities that a Rainmaker performs. You'll notice it's not listed as one of the five roles. Does that make sense?"

"It does. I've never liked the idea of being pigeonholed as either a Hunter *or* a Farmer, so I'm actually glad to hear you say that."

"Good. So, let's go back to the Hunter role. One thing that will help us look at each of these roles is a 'definition' or description that illustrates the characteristics of someone who excels in the role. While there is much more depth behind each of them, let's look at the 'high points' behind the Hunter practice."

She displayed another slide.

HUNTER

- Is a self-starter
- Seeks out problems and opportunities
- Displays intense curiosity
- Uses a "system" to keep the pipeline full
- Actively qualifies for potential and resources
- Connects and networks with all influencers

"So, as you suggested, a Hunter is someone who is always looking for that next opportunity. They are very self-motivated.

- In fact, the first characteristic of Hunters is that they are 'self-starters.' They don't need to be pushed by their manager - they *want* it and they go after it.
- They are always seeking out *problems*, which lead to *opportunities* where they can provide value.
- Hunters are intensely curious and want to know more – to find 'pains' that other salespeople may not notice and they seek out the internal champions and decision-makers.
- They often use a 'system' to help them manage their business and keep the pipeline full. They might, for example, schedule two specific hours a day – every day – to call new prospects. They're very protective of their 'selling time' and they never let anything interfere with it.

- They qualify opportunities early in the sales process to ensure they are working with those that have strong potential.
- And they are constantly connecting and networking to meet more people.

"Given that description, Ryan, can you think of anyone that you would describe as a Hunter?"

Ryan thought for a few moments.

"Yes, but the person I'm thinking of doesn't work at Summers. He's a college friend of mine who now works for an investment company. He's always selling – but he's a bit too aggressive for my style."

"I understand. Let's be clear – being a good Hunter *does* mean you are aggressively seeking new business opportunities, but your style does *not* have to be aggressive. Actually a much better trait for a Hunter to have is *persistence*. The best Hunters I know are those that persevere even when others have given up. Does that apply to your friend?"

"It does. Even though he's a bulldog sometimes, he never gives up."

"That's true. Hunters are disciplined – they press on when the going gets tough."

Valerie continued. "I'd like you to think about someone else we both know who has some of the best qualities of an excellent Hunter. You mentioned this person the other day when we first talked."

"Oh? Who's that?"

"James Miller. You talked about him coming from the competition recently and how he is now outselling most of the long-term people at Summers."

"Oh, right," said Ryan. "But he doesn't strike me as what I think of as a Hunter. I've worked with him on a couple of things and he seems like just an average, run-of-the-mill guy."

"Yes," said Valerie, "an average, run-of-the-mill guy who happens to be one of the best networkers I've ever known! I met him at an industry function in Reno a few years ago, and I remember thinking at the time that he was getting to know all the most important people at the conference. We connected several more times over the years. I was somewhat instrumental in bringing him to Summers because he made such an impression on me."

"Really? I had no idea."

"He's a guy who is almost on a 'mission' to share the benefits of our products and services – and he is *always* prospecting. One thing I really like is his key belief about building business: he takes full responsibility for his own success. He doesn't let the economy, or the competition, or the challenges of day-to-day business keep him from driving towards his goals.

"But what he also does very well is know how to go after the 'right' customers – the decision-makers, the internal champions within a company. He's a master at 'managing the white space' if you know what I mean."

"Actually, I *don't* know what you mean. What is 'managing the white space?'"

"Let me see if I can draw something that will help describe what that means." She began to draw on a sheet of paper.

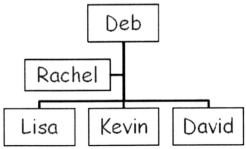

"You see this organization chart? When we're involved in a complex organization, we use this to try to understand the customer's hierarchy, don't we?"

"Yes, sometimes."

"Do you see all the 'white space' that surrounds the org chart?"

"Yes... where is this going?"

"Where it's going is this. In a large organization (and sometimes in a small company), good salespeople ask their customer for an org chart when they are first calling on them. It helps to see the structure of the business. But I always told my team members to *draw their own org chart* after a meeting and keep filling it in and adding to it as they learn more about the company. What I found is that people and titles often change...many company org charts get out of date pretty quickly."

She continued. "The best Hunters *ask, network, research,* and do whatever it takes to 'fill in the white space' on the chart. Who reports to whom? Who is really behind an initiative? Who are the key advisors? Who are the gatekeepers that can give you access or prevent you from seeing the decision makers? *All of it* should end up on your org chart."

"Look, here's one I did using some software I found. I was even able to get pictures of several people which helped me remember them when I saw them in person. I would study this before I went to the customer site."

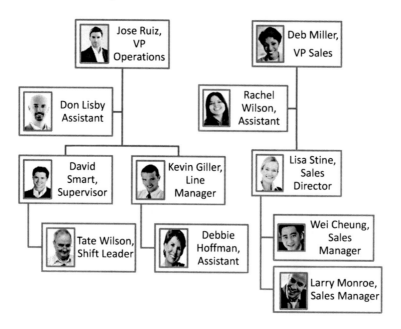

"Have you ever created your own org chart like this, Ryan?"

He studied the page that Valerie showed him. He could see that there were far more players on this chart than he knew for most of his customers.

"I've done simple ones many times. But to this level? No, I'd have to say I haven't been doing that."

"You should try it. You'll be surprised at how much further you can get by meeting more people in the company. So filling in the org chart at a deeper level is the first step of 'managing the white space.'

"The second step is to meet and get to know these people – to 'work' the customer's company. And I don't mean just your key contacts. I mean their assistant, their peers, other influencers… the list goes on. Rainmakers know that the assistant has two daughters who both play elite-level soccer, for example. Is learning this kind of information something you've tried to do?"

"Certainly with my primary contacts, I do. I pride myself on learning as much as I can about my customers and trying to find something in common with them that we can talk about. It works pretty well."

"Good. Unfortunately, I've seen too many salespeople that don't know much about anyone besides their one or two primary contacts. That's a huge mistake. If their primary contact leaves, they're often left behind. Managing the white spaces like this pays off in droves."

"I can see I need to go deeper. But surely you don't mean that I should be doing this for *all* my customers?"

"In an ideal world, you would. But as we both know, there are only so many hours in a day. The trick is to make the most of the hours that you do have."

"So how do I decide which customers to 'work' harder?"

"Great question. And it leads me to a little story. When I began in sales many years ago, I was very driven and I tried to go after any and every opportunity with the same gusto. The competitor in me really wanted to win them all. But I was getting frustrated because I didn't seem to be getting the 'big' deals that some of my colleagues were."

She continued. "A new manager joined our group at about that time – he had a tremendous impact on my career. He told me, *"Val, if you've got 100 prospects, I want you to get rid of 80 of them!"*

"Really?" Ryan looked puzzled.

"I was as surprised as you when he made that statement, but it really stuck with me over the years. What you want to hunt for are *good* customers – the ones with the most potential. If you want to be a Rainmaker, you simply cannot chase every piece of business."

"I can see that, but what's the best way to make those decisions?"

"Good Hunters use several different criteria to determine which opportunities to pour their efforts into."

Valerie pulled out a notepad and wrote some points.

- *What are my strongest opportunities?*
- *Where can I win?*
- *Where can I leverage previous success stories?*
- *Where is the greatest potential?*

"To put it another way," said Valerie, "You want to go *deep* instead of *wide*. Pick the customers where you have the best chance of winning bigger pieces of business and make them your primary focus."

"That seems like it's easier said than done," said Ryan.

"It takes some effort – but it has big payoffs. I'm going to show you a tool used by some of the best Hunters I know. It's called an 'ABCD' grid. Does that ring any bells with you?"

"No, I haven't heard of that one."

"The 'ABCD' grid is a great tool I used regularly and encouraged my team members to use. It helps you make deliberate choices; it provides *focus* and helps you determine which customers are the ones where you should invest most of your time."

Valerie opened a file folder on the desk and pulled out a sheet of paper saying, "There are several different 'flavors' of these grids, but the one I use looks like this."

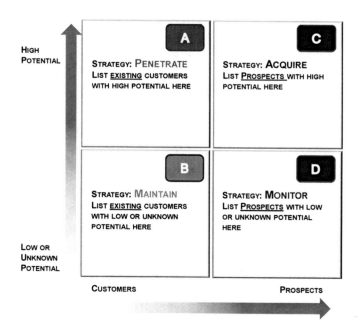

She let Ryan study the sheet for a moment and then said, "As you can see, there are four blocks in the grid – A, B, C, and D. If you look at the vertical axis, you can see that the lower blocks represent customers with 'low' or 'unknown' potential – so those with higher potential are the 'A' and 'C' blocks.

She continued. "On the horizontal axis, the two blocks on the left – the 'A' and 'B' blocks – represent current customers while those on the right – the 'C' and 'D' blocks – represent prospects that we are targeting. "

"So let's think about how you can use this grid to help you determine where to focus.

- In the 'A' block, you list *existing* customers with *high* potential – the strategy for these customers is to Penetrate them.
- In the 'B' block, you list *existing* customers with *lower* potential – you don't want to lose these customers but you don't see much room for growth – the strategy for these customers is to Maintain them.
- In the 'C' block, you list prospects with high potential – the strategy here is to Acquire them.
- And finally, in the 'D' block, you list prospects with low or unknown potential. The strategy for these prospects is to Monitor them.

She looked at Ryan and asked him, "If you had to pick two of these to focus on, which would you select?

Ryan looked at the chart closely. "The ones with higher potential – the 'A' and 'C' blocks."

"That's right. Good Hunters are all about *penetrating* their current customers with high potential and *acquiring* prospects with high potential. The problem is, many salespeople put equal amounts of time and effort into all four blocks! They're working hard, always on the go, but they haven't really focused on the 'ROI' – the *return on investment* of their energy."

Ryan thought about his earlier conversation with Luis and how this reinforced his new strategy.

"You know," said Ryan, "in talking with Luis the other day, he called himself a 'mole.' He said he keeps working through the layers of his customers until he's met people in most of the departments or divisions – and he often earns their business as well."

"That's obviously worked very well for Luis. He targets the high-potential customers in the 'A' block on the grid. And I'll bet he 'manages the white spaces' of those companies very well. Because he's also so dedicated to service excellence, he's able to maintain the customers in his 'B' block – he keeps them happy and coming back for more."

Ryan studied the grid again. "I think I could be one of the people guilty of going after most customers with the same 'gusto,' as you put it. I know I work very hard at getting any and all sales."

"It's part of the progression of a good salesperson. When you first start in sales 'all business is good business' as the saying goes. But as a top salesperson progresses, they learn that all business is not equal and the Rainmakers have learned how to block out the noise, so to speak. They know their products and services provide real value to their customers and they are disciplined to find the 'best' opportunities for both parties."

Valerie looked at the clock. "We've gone over the amount of time that I had planned for today – time really does fly when you're having fun, I guess!"

Ryan laughed. "Fun isn't how I'd describe it...yet. But helpful, meaningful, valuable... I'm so appreciative for this time you're spending with me."

"Not at all. Here's what I suggest you do before we meet next week. Why don't you take an evening or two to try to place the customers and prospects on your target list in one of the blocks on the grid. Then when you come back we'll talk about what you found."

"Sounds great. See you next week."

Ryan left the meeting on Hunter knowing the time he spent with Valerie could have a huge impact on his career. But he also knew it was up to him to make what he learned 'come alive.' When he got home from the meeting, he immediately began putting his target customers and prospects into the 'ABCD' grid to see where he stood.

Two days later...

Hearing a light knock on her office door, Valerie looked up and was surprised to see Ryan carrying a flowering plant from the local farmer's market.

"Hello!" she said. "Did I get my dates wrong? I wasn't expecting you today."

"No, I just came by to thank you. I think you may have started me on the path towards making rain."

"Oh? Have a seat. I want to hear your thoughts."

Ryan began. "When I left here the other day, I went home and started plotting my target customers on the 'ABCD' grid. I knew I'd have to be very honest in assessing where these companies fit on the grid. When I finished, to my dismay, I realized that two-thirds of them fell into the 'B' and 'D' blocks. Take a look."

Ryan pulled out the grid where he had listed his top 30 customers and prospects.

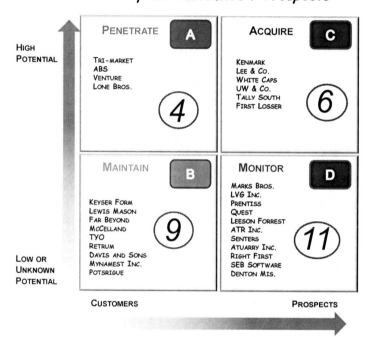

Top 30 Customers / Prospects

"Unfortunately, I had to conclude that I'm spending a lot of time and energy going after companies with 'low or unknown potential' on the lower half of the grid. I'm pursuing a lot of prospects but when I really started to evaluate things and ask myself some of the questions you brought up last week – like 'where can I win?' – I had to admit that much of my effort may be misplaced."

He continued. "One of my biggest concerns is that I have so many customers – and spend a lot of time – in the 'B' block – *existing customers with low growth potential.* As the strategy states, I want to 'maintain' these customers – they're doing a lot of business with us – but I have to acknowledge that they don't have a large potential for future growth. How do you balance that? We certainly don't want to lose them."

"That's a great observation," said Valerie. "It's very true that you'll have some big customers who do a lot of business and require frequent maintenance – yet have low potential for future growth. And you're right – those customers are very important to Summers' business.

"However, if the growth potential is not really there, Rainmakers recruit other people from their own company to help service those customers. This frees up more time for you to focus on opportunities where there *is* more growth potential. It's very easy to get bogged down in areas where you aren't making the best use of your time. Rainmakers are aware of that. We'll talk more about how to recruit others in another session."

Ryan listened intently. "I'll look forward to hearing more about how to make that transition."

"Meanwhile," said Ryan, "I did something else yesterday that you'll appreciate. I recognize that it's easier to meet with my established customers – the contacts I already have a relationship with – but I started scoping out the 'white spaces' for some of the companies I'm calling on. I like the idea of completing my own org chart so I started one for four of my customers already. I'm getting excited about the possibilities!"

"That's terrific. Hunting is an area where many people struggle – so I'm glad that you're excited about it. The best Rainmakers are exceptional Hunters. And *managing the white spaces* and using the *ABCD grid* are two good ways to help you get on track towards stronger and more valuable hunting opportunities."

Ryan nodded. "I agree. One more thing... how often should I update my ABCD grid?"

"I used to update mine every six months or so – you want it to be current. Some people update it more often but for me, that worked out pretty well. I would also update the org charts regularly – whenever I learned something new or found out about a change."

"That sounds reasonable," said Ryan. "Well, I don't want to keep you – I knew I was taking a chance dropping by, but I was in the area, so I thought I'd bring you up to speed on what I've been doing."

"I'm glad you did. By the way, yesterday I called James Miller – the 'Hunter' we talked about. We had a good conversation and I told him about how you and I are working on defining the roles of a Rainmaker. He said he'll be here in town for a meeting in two weeks. I suggested the three of us get together for dinner if he could work it into his schedule and he immediately agreed. He's also a big believer in sharing ideas."

"Wow – that's great. I'll really look forward to that."

"Me too. Can you check your calendar and make sure you're free on the 19th? I was thinking we could try that new seafood place on Market Street."

Ryan checked his mobile calendar. "That works for me," he said. "Michelle will be jealous – I told her we'd go there soon."

"She's welcome to join us. But I don't know how much she would enjoy the conversation," laughed Valerie.

"That's okay - I'll check it out and she and I will go another time. She'll be happy to hear about this collaboration. She's a big 'continuous learner' herself."

"I knew I liked her," laughed Valerie.

Key Ideas from Hunter Chapter

- Using the White Space Key Players Worksheet**
- Focusing on Potential
- Establish focus via the ABCD Opportunity Grid**

**These tools can be found starting on page 157 and online at www.saleseffectiveness.com/rainmaker

CHAPTER NOTES

_____

_____

_____

_____

_____

_____

"Rainmakers are akin to investigative reporters, detectives, psychiatrists, doctors, and archaeologists. They ask, probe, dig, diagnose, and listen."

Jeffrey J. Fox

Chapter 7

CONSULTANT

When Ryan came to her office for their next meeting, Valerie began with an apology. "I don't think I properly thanked you for the plant. Look...it's still blooming beautifully. It was a nice gesture and it reinforced something I already knew … you have a trait that is held by most Rainmakers."

"What's that?" asked Ryan.

"A spirit of genuine caring. As I said earlier, people tend to buy from someone they *like*, *know*, and *trust*, and customers can tell if someone is not authentic. Your thoughtful attentiveness will take you a long way with customers. You can learn *skills* from others but *attitudes* must be cultivated from within."

"Thank you," said Ryan. "To tell you the truth, that's part of why I went into sales. When I was younger, I always thought of salespeople as being pushy... kind of obnoxious people. But then a friend of our family – a man who was very successful in sales – told me it's the exact opposite. That the best salespeople are in the business because they care about people and want to help them. That idea stuck with me when I was thinking about a career."

"Your friend had it right," said Valerie. "Unfortunately not everyone has come to that realization. But top salespeople are the ones who can really put themselves in their customers' shoes. How do they feel? What keeps them up at night? What makes them tick? If you can 'live' in your customer's skin, and demonstrate sincere empathy for their situation, you go much further than others who don't have that ability."

"I learned a lot about empathy from watching my dad," said Ryan. "Over the years I've realized that he can really sense what other people are feeling. I've seen how he reads people's emotions and how that helps him connect to them – he's very genuine and he seems to always know how to respond in any situation. I've always tried to emulate him in that way."

"And by the way," he said, "the plant is the least I could do – I've gained so much from our meetings already. The way you're giving your time to me reinforces why you've been so successful. I certainly feel that you've put yourself in *my* shoes!"

"It doesn't seem that long ago that I *was* in your shoes," laughed Valerie. "So are you ready to start talking about the Consultant role?"

"I am."

"Before we begin, let's go back one more time to the five roles of a Rainmaker." She opened the slide.

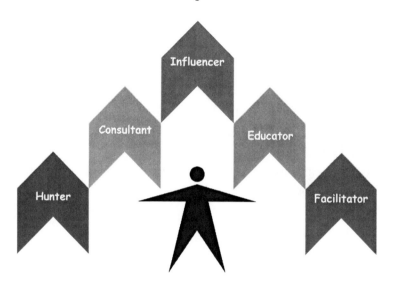

"I've been thinking," said Valerie, "about a new way – a simple way – to view the roles:

- Hunting *identifies* opportunities.
- Consulting, Influencing, and Educating *turn the opportunities into business*.
- And Facilitating *ensures we deliver on our commitments* in order to build customer loyalty.

Does that help convey the meaning of the roles for you at a high level?"

"That's interesting," said Ryan. "I'm beginning to see the picture. I agree that could be a good way to communicate the Rainmaker roles."

"Right. Put them all together and 'Wow!' – there's the magic we talked about."

She continued. "So last week we talked about Hunter – the role that helps us identify opportunities. Now the first of the roles that will help turn opportunities into business is the Consultant role. You told me when we first met that you've done some research on this topic. What did you learn?"

"I learned that one of the keys to being a consultative salesperson is to ask better questions that help you understand a customer's problems and business issues. As a new salesperson, I used to go in and do much more 'telling' than 'asking.' I now know that asking encourages the customer to talk more. The more they talk the more I learn."

"Very true. Good Consultants follow the '90/10' rule – asking questions and listening intently 90% of the time, and *telling* only 10% of the time. Here's another expression some salespeople really need to hear: *'You have two ears and only one mouth – you should be listening twice as much as talking.'* Have you heard that expression?"

Ryan laughed. "Not in those words. But I've been working very hard at it lately."

"Excellent," said Valerie. "Asking strong questions is definitely part of consulting. But there's much more to it that often gets overlooked. For example, what kind of research do you typically do on your customers?"

"I check their web site, but in reality, many times I do very little research prior to a call. I just don't feel like I have the time."

"Part of that may be due to the issue we talked about earlier – targeting too many customers at one time. However, a true consultative salesperson *always* researches as much as possible about the company and the people they're calling on prior to a call. Have you heard the term 'due diligence?'"

"Yes, I've heard it used generally by lawyers and such."

"Right. The term 'due diligence' is used a lot by people in professional services like lawyers and CPA's to refer to their duty to exercise *care* in any transaction. It involves investigating all aspects of a target company they're dealing with. The term sounds a little lofty but it really translates into a couple of basic factors they use to ensure success – 'doing their homework' and 'thinking things through.' Conducting due diligence – or thorough research – is a habit practiced by good consultative salespeople as well."

"What are the best ways to conduct due diligence?"

"Starting with a company's web site is the easiest, most obvious technique. And, as you know, some companies have terrific web sites where you can learn a lot, while others are very weak. So, beginning there is fine; just be aware that there are many other options that a lot of people don't think about."

"Like…?"

"Like searching for them on some of the popular social networking sites. Sometimes the company itself has its own social networking account where they post more current, up-to-the minute news than you will ever find on their official web site. Many companies keep their web sites fairly static. On the other hand, social network sites are updated frequently – I'm guessing you use some of them yourself?"

"I do. But I've never thought of using them to engage with my customers."

"Try it. I think you'll find some interesting information that your competitors won't think to access. And have you seen some of the new apps for your mobile device? I think this is the direction a lot of companies are going to go – they can make immediate offers to their customers based on things like their location and habits. The world of technology is influencing almost everything we do these days and we absolutely must take advantage of the information we find."

"How do you feel about using a company's annual report as a source of information?"

Valerie responded. "Sure – they can be a powerful resource and you can often find them online now. The annual report is a good way to help you learn about the company's activities, future plans and forecasts. I always try to see if the CEO has a letter in the report about the direction he or she wants to take the company. There's also the '10-K' report that can be very enlightening if you're working with a large customer. Are you familiar with it?"

"No. What is it?"

"A 10-K report is an official financial report filed annually by public companies with the SEC. It provides detailed financial information, a list of their different divisions, their subsidiaries, and even legal proceedings the company is involved in. It can provide a wealth of information."

"I believe it," said Ryan. "And let's not forget the company's marketing collateral – I often read it to see what I can learn about their new products and services."

"Absolutely. All of these things provide excellent insight into the customer's world – their business issues, their challenges, where they're headed. Great consultants have intense curiosity about their customers."

"And a Consultant uses that insight to prepare their questions, right?" said Ryan.

"Right. Good, thought-provoking questions are the basis for having 'meaningful conversations' with customers. And a 'meaningful conversation' is much more than just talking with them. Let me ask you… right now, what kind of questions do you typically ask your customers?"

"Well," said Ryan, "it depends what stage of the sales cycle we're in, but for new customers, I may ask, *'What's been happening in your business lately?'* or *'What is preventing you from growing more?'* Things like that."

Valerie paused. "Try to think about how you could ask a more targeted question to a customer after you've spent time researching them."

"Let's see" said Ryan. "Okay, how's this? *'I did some research and found that your company is getting very involved in environmental issues. How has that initiative impacted your operations?'"*

"Great example! I like it! That question provokes critical thinking. Your earlier questions were okay but they sounded more like you were 'fishing' for information. Do you see the difference?"

"I do. I can see how the customer would be more inclined to want to have this conversation."

"Good consultative sales pros become 'students' of questions. They build a library of great questions that challenge the customer to *think* and *self-discover*. I remember one of the best salespeople on one of my teams developed over 250 questions, with 5 to 10 questions for each of the problems that customers often experience."

"I've never thought of having a database of questions," said Ryan. "Did he use all of them?"

"At one time or another, probably yes. He carried many of the questions with him, using them as 'thought joggers' to help him plan his calls. He'd review the database ahead of time and have at least 5 to 7 targeted questions planned to use on any call."

"Interesting," said Ryan.

"It was always a wonderful experience riding along on calls with him. I'd pick up great questions every time."

She continued. "Consultants know that having strong questions prepared is a good *first* step. But the second step is what distinguishes an average salesperson from a Rainmaker – and that step involves the 'depth' of the person's questioning."

"The depth?" asked Ryan.

"Yes. What I've noticed is that many people ask what I call 'the top layer' of questions very well. But it's the *deeper* and *richer* questions that come as a follow on to the 'top layer' questions that really bring out the issues – the 'need behind the need,' if you will."

"Like what?"

"Rather than me trying to define them, let's act out a typical scenario, using a technique called *'why, why, why.'* Are you game?"

"Sure. How do we do that?"

"Once a top layer question is answered, strong Consultants ask 'why?' – up to three times – to find the root cause of a situation. Pretend I'm a customer and ask me a typical question you might ask on an early sales call. Then I want you to ask me at least two more *'why's'* to dig deeper. Let's see how it goes."

"Okay," Ryan began. "Valerie, what are the challenges you're facing in achieving your goals next year?"

She replied, "I think the biggest challenge we'll face next year is order fulfillment."

She paused, then said, "I'm going to step out of my role for a second, but I want to make a point right here. A lot of salespeople would stop after my answer and move on to something else or immediately try to demonstrate how their product or service can help solve my issue – order fulfillment. Instead, I want you to probe deeper – try to ask at least two more '*why's*' around my answer."

"Okay," said Ryan. "Why do you think that order fulfillment is going to be an issue next year?"

"In January, we're going to start taking orders from overseas and I'm concerned that we'll have problems dealing with the red tape of importing and exporting."

She nodded to Ryan to ask another '*why*' question.

"And why do you think this will affect order fulfillment?" he asked.

She replied, "All of our competitors use an outside organization to handle their Customs paperwork. To save costs, we're going to try to handle it ourselves. But so far we haven't really figured out all the ins and outs."

Ryan smiled at Valerie. "I see what you're saying. If I had stopped after the first or second question, I may have thought your order fulfillment issue had to do with production, or labor, or something else."

"Right. Believe me, this happens all the time. We *think* we know what the customer is talking about, so we move on, or we go down a bunny trail. Good

Consultants don't do that – they dig and dig until they uncover the customer's *real* drivers, needs, and issues."

Ryan said, "I agree that most of the salespeople I know primarily ask the 'top-level' questions – myself included."

"The importance of understanding the root of an issue came out strongly in the past few years with a renewed emphasis by businesses on 'quality' – introducing things like Six Sigma in workplace environments. A lot of businesses are using root problem analysis in their production and operations divisions but only recently has it made its way into sales. Digging deeper is really at the heart of quality sales consulting."

"Are there any other tools you use to help with this?" asked Ryan.

"Yes. The tool I like is called a 'fishbone' analysis. It's a very simple concept where you draw a 'fish' with a head and four 'fish bones' coming off of the body. Let me draw a quick example."

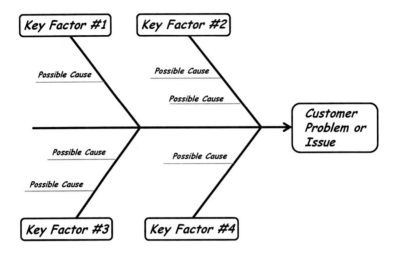

Valerie said, "I'm not a great artist, but can you see how this resembles a fish with its 'bones'?"

Ryan smiled. "I can. So this helps you identify the possible root cause of an issue or problem?"

"It does. It's a straightforward way to help you dig deeper – with your customers, your manager, or in any situation where you want to get a better understanding of an issue. I use it with customers a lot or in team meetings to help identify underlying causes of an issue."

"I haven't seen this before. Is it something I could use in a customer meeting?"

"Ideally, yes, you would draw it out with the customer during a meeting, asking targeted questions to help fill in the factors that are impacting the problem or business issue you are discussing. When it's laid out this way, it provides a lot of clarity on the issue and most customers love it. It's very easy to use and many people have never seen something like it before. If you do it well, it can really help customers begin to see you as a Consultant."

"I like it," said Ryan.

Valerie said, "There's just one more area I'd like to explore before we leave the Consultant role."

"What's that?"

"It's the idea of using written communications to differentiate yourself and to keep momentum going with your customers. Let me ask you, do you ever send an *agenda* before a customer meeting or create a written meeting *summary* after a meeting?"

"No, generally not."

"I've found that most salespeople don't do these things. However, good Consultants generally do. Taking these two simple steps – sending the customer an agenda and writing up a call summary or recap – can really set us apart from our competitors. In addition to helping make customer meetings very productive and focused, they keep you 'top of mind' with your customers who begin to see you differently than they see other salespeople."

Ryan wondered aloud, "I'm thinking Carmen – one the other Rainmakers we talked about – may do this. I attended a training session with her last summer and we were at the same table. In the morning before the session began, she said she was drafting an agenda for an upcoming customer meeting. During the workshop I realized what a strong salesperson she was and I meant to ask her about it later, but I never got around to it."

"Why don't you try to reach out to her sometime? She strikes me as another person that would be happy to share tips and ideas. Find out what she tries to include in her communications and what kind of results she gets."

"Good idea. And I'll bring her up to speed on what we're doing to see if she has any other ideas for us."

"Great. So, before you go, let's recap. Just as for Hunter, I've tried to summarize the key characteristics of a salesperson who is a strong Consultant. Take a look."

CONSULTANT

- Acts as a 'change agent' to the customer
- Thinks analytically and anticipates trends
- Is able to see the BIG picture
- Thinks like an owner – helps the customer see how they can grow their business
- Seen as a problem solver
- Always uses sound judgment
- Keeps aware of industry direction

Valerie paused while Ryan read through the bullets shown on the slide.

"As we discussed, a sales professional wearing the Consultant hat becomes an expert in understanding the customer's business. Consultants promote positive change for the customer and use analytical skills to try to gain complete insight into the company's culture and perspective. They anticipate the future and offer the customer *objective* thinking – not as someone trying to 'sell' their products and services, but as a genuine advisor that is looking out for the customer's best interest."

She continued. "A Consultant sees the big picture of the business and tries to really understand the customer's goals for the business. They think like 'owners' and they make their comments and suggestions from that frame of reference. They seek to identify and solve problems the customer may be experiencing– problems the customer sometimes didn't even know they had. And they always use sound judgment and absolute integrity."

Ryan replied. "I see now that there's much more to being a Consultant than just asking good questions."

"Exactly. Rainmakers can actually help set a customer's direction and even help them turn around if they're going in the wrong direction. They know what's happening in the industry and customers value and look forward to working with them."

"Thank you. Once again, I really got a lot out of this meeting. Where would you like to meet next week?"

"Actually, " said Valerie, "My husband and I are heading to the beach next weekend. Could you meet at The Red Barn for an early breakfast on Friday morning?"

"Sure – that'll work, but would you rather put it off a week?"
"No, I think we should keep the momentum going. We're planning for a relaxing trip but I'm sure I'll be thinking about the five roles so this will keep them fresh in my mind. Next week we'll talk about the third hat you'll be wearing as a Rainmaker – INFLUENCER."

Key Ideas from the Consultant Chapter

- Following the 90/10 Rule
- Using annual reports and 10K reports
- Having a database of powerful questions**
- Using the Why-Why-Why technique
- Applying a Fishbone Analysis**

**These tools can be found starting on page 157 and online at www.saleseffectiveness.com/rainmaker

CHAPTER NOTES

"To influence may be the highest level of human skills."

Anonymous

Chapter 8

INFLUENCER

Ryan was looking forward to his meeting with Valerie on the Influencer role. He believed most top salespeople possess contagious enthusiasm and have a natural ability to 'win people over' which was a big reason for their desire to go into sales as a career. *"You could sell dirt to worms"* he'd been told as a young boy. He thought that the Influencer role was probably where he would most use this natural ability.

He arrived at The Red Barn in plenty of time to get a table and drink a cup of coffee before Valerie arrived – or so he thought. Walking in to the restaurant, he spotted her sitting at a quiet table near the back.

"Aren't you the early bird!" Ryan laughed as he approached the table. "I thought I'd be here first."

"Good morning!" said Valerie, gesturing for him to sit down. "I woke up early to finish packing. Then I realized

I don't have much to take since we plan on mostly reading and relaxing, so it went quicker than I thought."

"I really hope meeting this morning isn't too much of an imposition," said Ryan. "Right before your vacation."

"No, it's fine. Everything's set and our flight isn't till 10 o'clock so we have plenty of time."

Valerie studied Ryan's face. "How are you feeling about things? Making progress?"

"I'm feeling better. I think the roles are starting to take hold for me. I think I'm making progress on the Consultant role – I'm spending more time on due diligence for my key prospects and I'm digging deeper in meetings. In fact, I think a few opportunities may have opened up as a result of asking better follow-on questions. I really like using the 'three why's' technique."

"In fact," he said, "I told my wife the other day that when I'm going into some of my calls now, I feel like I have a 'little Valerie' on my shoulder, coaching me along."

Valerie laughed as their waitress appeared. "I'll blow my calorie count today and go for the house special," she said, handing her menu to the waitress.

"Make it two," said Ryan. "I'm planning to run later tonight so I'll put in an extra mile or two."

Valerie began. "Okay. Before our food comes, let's talk about the Influencer role. What are your thoughts around that word?"

"I think the word 'influence' is one of the more motivational words in selling. Great salespeople like to persuade and win people over. Is that how you see it?" asked Ryan.

"Partly. The word *influence* comes from the Latin word *influere* which means to 'flow into' – in this case, it's the ability of a person to be a compelling force on the actions of others. I do agree with you, that most salespeople enjoy the challenges associated with 'winning people over;' if they didn't, I'm not sure they'd be right for a career in sales. The key is, however, that the salesperson shouldn't be persuading customers *against their will,* so to speak, but always trying to build the desire, or the 'want to' from the customer's perspective."

She continued. "Have you ever heard this expression? *'Nobody wants to be sold, but everyone wants to buy.'*"

Ryan replied, "I haven't, but it makes sense. I know it's true for me! Maybe it's because I'm in sales myself, but I can sense a salesperson trying to 'sell' me a mile away. And it does bother me when they try to do so by promoting what they offer before determining what I am looking for. But I *do* like to buy things from a salesperson that seems to really understand my needs and concerns."

"Exactly. It's all about the *like, know and trust* factors we mentioned earlier. These factors really come out in the Influencer role."

"What do you mean?" asked Ryan.

"Early in my sales career, I became very interested in what it is about salespeople that affects their level of *influence* on customers – that helps customers *want* to buy. As I was developing my own sales style, I realized that there are many different approaches people use. At first I thought it was just a 'personality' or 'charisma' thing, but I decided to do some research on *influencing* and *persuasion*. What I found was fascinating!"

"What did you find?"

"There's a great deal of *science* behind the art of influencing. Probably the best-known professional on the topic is a man named Robert Cialdini who wrote a book called *Influence – The Psychology of Persuasion*. This book really helped my sales career."

"Hmmm… I've never heard of it in all the sales stuff I've read."

Valerie laughed. "I know – it's not one of the standard books people in sales pick up. However, you might want to take a look at it sometime. The book opened my eyes to six principles of persuasion:

- Reciprocity
- Scarcity
- Liking
- Authority
- Social proof
- Commitment

She continued. "For example, I learned that one of the main reasons many customers decide to buy is based on the principle of '*social proof*.'"

"I'm not familiar with that term."

"Social proof means that we often determine what is correct by finding out what *other* people think is correct. It's why so many companies use celebrities for TV commercials. In sales, social proof is applied through *testimonials*. Do you have a library of testimonials that you use?"

"A library? Well, I carry some letters we've been given by customers, and some of our marketing materials contain quotes from customers. Is that what you mean?"

"That's a start. The company tries to provide you with tools and materials to help your sales efforts. But the most powerful testimonials I ever got were the ones I collected myself – from my own customers. These provided a convincing argument to my prospects when they had doubts about working with Summers – or with me. There is no better way to relieve people's concerns than seeing and feeling what other people experienced."

Valerie reached into a folder and pulled out an example – a letter from one of her customers. "Here's one from one of my long-term customers – a VP for a large firm in Charlotte. A letter like this is worth its weight in gold as a selling tool for new customers."

Ryan read the letter, written on the customer's stationery and signed by the VP.

*During the past year, we have worked with Summers Inc.
and specifically with Valerie Monroe to establish a more
efficient process model for our Operations division. We
evaluated many companies prior to making a buying
decision; our choice to go with Summers was largely based
on Valerie's thorough and professional evaluation of our
current issues and our confidence in her ability to see us
through the entire change process. She established
credibility with our entire team and her assessment of the
value that her solutions would provide was 'spot on.'*

*Valerie was very tactful and diplomatic in challenging our
thinking and she helped us develop a strategy that has paid
huge dividends not only for our division and our company
but also for our customers. In addition to understanding
the issues that drove our need for change, Valerie helped us
anticipate the potential outcomes of our decisions. We
estimate a 300% return on our investment to date and the
benefits continue as our market share increases. Valerie
and Summers have my highest endorsement.*

"Wow," said Ryan. "I can see why you say this is worth
its weight in gold. Did the customer write this on his
own?"

"Yes. He wrote it on his own, although I did request that
he write it. I've developed the habit of *asking* for a
written testimonial from many of my best customers. It
seemed awkward at first but it became very easy. For the
most part, assuming your work has been good, people
want to help you if they're asked – we just forget to ask!"

Ryan recalled his conversation with Michelle about asking Valerie for help. He was hesitant to do so then, but it was one of the best decisions he'd ever made.

"So how should I go about this?" asked Ryan.

"Well, you need to first make it a habit to ask, particularly after you had an exceptionally positive experience with a customer."

She continued. "Before asking, though, think about what occurred. What problems did you help solve? What pain did you take away? What financial impact did your solution have? How easy were you to work with? You will be able to share these ideas when the customer asks you for some ideas on what to include in the letter."

"Did you ever get letters like this without asking?"

"Only a few – most people rarely think about doing it. How many times have you actually written a letter of commendation for someone – even when you've been given excellent service or attention? But if the person *asked* you, and if that person also gave you some ideas of what to say…"

"I get it. Make it easy for them."

"Right. A couple of times, customers even asked me to draft the entire letter for them. They signed it, of course, and verified it was all true, but no one knows better than you about the work you put in and the value you provide. Those were some fun letters to write!"

"I know exactly who I'm going to ask," said Ryan. "I finished up a good-sized project with a customer this week that took a lot of extra time and effort on my part. I feel certain that Jack will write me a testimonial."

"I'm sure he will," said Valerie. "Before we continue, let's look quickly at the key characteristics of an Influencer."

INFLUENCER

- **Builds a library of testimonials to inspire customers to take action**
- **Understands how to demonstrate the financial benefits of their solution**
- **Uses stories to make ideas come to life**
- **Creates a "compelling reason to act"**
- **Persuades from the customer's perspective**
- **Negotiates successful outcomes**

After they looked at the characteristics, Valerie began. "So we've talked about testimonials and how important they can be to the Influencer practice. Let's now spend a few minutes exploring the next idea that's essential to your ability to influence your customers."

"What's that?" asked Ryan.

"I call it *'show me the money.'* You and I both know that in a financially-driven world, if a customer doesn't believe their company will save money – or make money – as a result of their decision... then there's often *no* decision. So a key part of *influencing* a customer to buy involves 'showing' them the money."

"Tell me about it," said Ryan. "That's all I seem to hear right now – '*I can get it cheaper from your competition*' or '*It's not in our budget.*'"

"Yes," said Valerie. "That feedback has been around throughout my entire career. And a problem I find is that many salespeople are not able to paint a clear picture to their customers around the *price* versus *true cost* of what they are selling. For example, most salespeople would say their product or service is 'more efficient' or 'faster' or 'stronger' or whatever it may be."

She continued. "And some customers have the intuitive ability to translate those words into how many dollars will actually be saved or how much it will help them grow. Let's say our product is actually faster than our competitor's similar product. However, because the customer doesn't know what 'faster' means in terms of real dollars, we are relegated to fighting a price war."

Ryan asked, "The *real* value is difficult to calculate, isn't it?"

"Sure, it can be. But there are tools that can help you determine the ROI (Return on Investment) or TCO (Total Cost of Ownership) for a customer. I suggest you spend some time investigating the options."

"Shouldn't our marketing group be doing that?"

"They may have information that can help in this area and often research is available that many salespeople don't make use of. The problem is, Marketing doesn't know the specifics around *your* customer… what solution they're currently using … how much they're paying… what their growth goals involve… what level of support will work the best for them."

She continued. "That means it's up to *you* to ask customers the right questions to help create the *dollarized value*. I think the most critical and most overlooked questions a salesperson can ask are *Consequences* questions. This is where you help customers *quantify* their issues. 'Digging deeper' when asking these questions has real meaning.

"Just for fun," said Valerie, "Let's practice a situation. Pretend I'm selling a solution to help a company be more productive in their call center. You be the customer and just respond to my questions with what you think could be reasonable answers."

"Okay," said Ryan.

She began. "So Mr. Customer, you've told me that the two issues you're most concerned with are dropped calls and the data analysis problems. Is that right?"

"Yes, those are our biggest issues – at least right now," said Ryan.

"So…on a scale of 1 to 10, with 1 being the least important issue and 10 being the most important issue, how would you rate these concerns?"

"Let's see. I'm going to say that the data analysis issue is a 4 and the dropped calls issue is a 9."

"Okay… let's talk about the dropped calls situation. Do you have any idea how much each dropped call is costing you?"

"I'd estimate that every dropped call is worth on average about $5 in lost revenue."

"And how many calls like that are there each day?"

"I'd say each of our 10 reps has about 10 per day."

"Okay," said Valerie. "So can we do the math together? If there are around 10 dropped calls per day for each rep, that's $500 per day, right? And, if they work 20 days a month, that's $10,000 a month, or $120,000 per year. And how many future customers might you be losing when a call is dropped?"

Ryan stepped out of character and smiled. "I see what you mean – this could go on for a while."

"Yes," said Valerie. "What you try to do is give the customer what is known as a 'compelling reason to act.' Many customers inwardly know they need to take action, but your questioning can provide that *compelling reason* – as you help them see exactly how much they stand to *gain* by acting on the information, or to *lose* by not acting on it.

"And how would you suggest I get started with this?"

"Do some research. Talk to the Marketing folks – they have a lot of information you can use in your meetings and presentations. And there are books and online tools that may help you develop your own approach to this.

"Remember," said Valerie. "What you're selling is not our products and services, but the *value* our customers receive by purchasing from us. Quantifying in terms of dollars and value creates that compelling reason to act – and gives you a huge leg up on the competition."

Valerie glanced at her watch.

"There's one more idea I want to touch on before we leave the Influencer role," said Valerie. "It may seem unusual, but this idea is how 'storytelling' can be one of the best skills you can develop to help influence people."

"Michelle says I tell stories all the time," laughed Ryan. "I think she's tired of hearing stories about my customers."

"Perfect. Storytelling is a wonderful technique used by top salespeople. It's one of the skills you should work on mastering. The best storyteller I know at Summers is Gary Lindner. At first glance, he's so quiet that you don't really expect it, but Gary absolutely enthralls customers with his stories – it's amazing to watch."

"No kidding?" Ryan was shocked. He knew Gary was one of the company's top sellers and he never really understood why. He had met him a couple of times at company functions and he seemed almost understated.

"Yes. Gary can deliver a story so well in a sales situation that before long the customer feels like they're old friends. Gary becomes more than a salesperson trying to sell them something; he's someone they *like, know and trust.* There it is again. They develop a bond and before you know it, they're buying. It's a skill I've somewhat developed but I'm still working to improve."

"Do you think it's a 'skill' you can learn?" asked Ryan.

"Why don't you try to contact Gary while I'm gone this week? Tell him about what we're doing and ask *him* that question. I think I know what he'll say but I also think it would be best for you to speak to him directly."

"Okay, I will." Ryan paused. "Before you leave, I wanted to ask you about how the skill of *negotiating* fits into the Influencer role. What are your thoughts on that?"

"There are different perspectives around negotiating. One camp believes that negotiation begins from your very first conversation with a customer. Others believe that negotiation should only occur once you've exhausted your selling skills and you run into an impasse. I believe both camps have merit but my personal bias is that a salesperson is responsible first for articulating the value of their company's products and services before beginning to negotiate."

Ryan asked, "But what happens when customers start a conversation with 'demands' that get you into negotiation early in the sales process?"

"It's my belief that if you study negotiation, it's really a deeper application of selling skills. There are lots of books on negotiation where you can find ideas on what works well for people. I personally have three key tips I keep in mind when I get into a negotiation situation. Send me a note and I'll email them to you if you'd like."

"Sounds good," said Ryan.

Ryan and Valerie finished their coffee and Valerie realized she'd have to hustle to pick up her husband in time for their flight.

"Have a great time!" said Ryan as he opened the door for Valerie.

Later that day...

That afternoon, Ryan sent Gary an email. He briefly described his meetings with Valerie and asked if Gary would mind spending a little time with him one evening during the week to talk about 'storytelling.' Gary readily agreed and told Ryan he'd call him Tuesday night.

When Ryan and Gary spoke on Tuesday, Gary seemed genuinely excited to talk about this subject.

"Learning to tell stories is something I worked at very hard earlier in my career," he said. "Now, it comes pretty naturally, but at the time, I had a mentor that was such a master storyteller, most customers actually looked forward to seeing him. He was one of the most successful salespeople in the company and I decided I wanted to be able to win customers over in the same way. So I researched the topic – at first just by watching and listening to him, and then by listening to other great storytellers on TV or in person. I even read a few books about how screenplay writers come up with stories – believe it or not, there are a lot of parallels those of us in sales can learn from professional storytellers."

He continued. "What I learned is that stories not only give the customer a lot of information, but also build energy and arouse their emotions.

"In fact," said Gary, "There's a good book called *'A Whole New Mind'* by Daniel Pink that affirmed for me the tremendous impact stories can make in business. He says that stories are a key way for people to distinguish their goods and services in a 'crowded marketplace.'"

"Interesting," said Ryan. "I love to tell stories but I didn't ever think about the fact that they could really help me grow business!"

"Good stories that customers can relate to can have a huge impact. And I even have a 'system' for my stories; I keep a file of potential ideas on my computer so that I can remember them and use them as needed. For years, I've been jotting down notes when something happens that I want to remember – just a few details so that I can practice the story and make it 'come to life' in a future customer situation."

"Really?" said Ryan. "I always thought people who did that were speaking 'off the cuff.'"

"Some can be more off the cuff than others. But think about it – do you know how many times a comedian rehearses to make it *seem* like he's telling a story spontaneously? It takes practice and you'll get much better quickly if you do indeed practice. I sometimes practice storytelling with my wife if she'll let me! I even tape myself occasionally just to see what I sound like – I don't want 'uh's' and 'um's' in my stories."

"One caveat," said Gary. You don't want to make a story seem memorized or over-rehearsed. Make sure you have fun along the way! Taking a Toastmasters' class helps many people – it's something you may want to think about."

"I'll look into it," said Ryan. "So what makes a good story?"

"The best stories always have some type of conflict or struggle – that's what makes them memorable and helps you influence customers. I often use a method I call 'SHARE,' to ensure I include the important elements when I *share* a story with a customer. These are:

- Situation – What was the situation?
- Hurdle – What obstacles were faced? What was the challenge? What conflicts arose?
- Action - What action was taken?
- Result – What was the end result?
- Evaluate – What were the lessons learned?"

"Can you give me an example?" asked Ryan.

"Sure. I used to sell commercial paint products before working at Summers. I was having some success with lots of small accounts but something happened fairly early in my career that made a huge difference for me."

He continued. "One day my wife went to visit an elderly aunt who had broken a hip and was staying temporarily in a nursing home – a good one we had seen for years. When my wife got there, she saw that the place was in pretty bad shape and really needed a refresh. She asked one of the nurses about it; the nurse said the patients couldn't tolerate the smell of paint and it was too difficult to move them, so the interior hadn't been painted in 15 years! They were losing business to newer facilities and although their services were top-notch, the nursing home was beginning to be seen as 'second tier.'

"My wife came home kind of down, and told me about it. Nursing homes were not on my radar for business, but our company had just come out with a low-odor paint that people found to be much less bothersome. So I made an appointment with the director and offered a demo for a non-patient room. After we painted it, they were astonished at the lack of odor. They even wheeled some patients in to the room to see if the smell bothered them and happily, no one had any problems.

"Well, guess what?" said Gary. "Not only did I get that contract – which really helped the nursing home improve its reputation – but that facility was owned by a company that had over 200 similar operations nationwide. It was one of my biggest sales ever and all because my wife visited her aunt one day."

He continued. "Even better, rather than just telling future customers in other industries that *'We have a low-odor paint,'* I began to tell that story. I could see my customers picturing their parents or grandparents staying in a place that was run down. They began to *see* the impact of low-odor and how it could be an important benefit in their environment too."

Ryan listened intently. "I see what you mean – that is a great story."

"Yes, it has all the elements – and I learned the importance of opening my mind to opportunities in all types of industries. Ever since, I've seen the value of connecting with customers through stories. They really leave a lasting impression."

"Hmmm….," said Ryan. "I've never fully explored all this. How can I learn more?"

"Here's what I suggest. Do some hands-on research yourself – listen to people, read about storytelling, even watch videos on a website called *TED-Ideas Worth Spreading* (ted.com) , or YouTube, or others. You'll learn a lot if you keep a *learning mindset*. Watch once for entertainment, and then watch a second and third time to study how the storyteller makes the story *come alive*.

"There's a lot of magic in good storytelling," said Gary, "and when you harness the magic, your customers will look forward to your visits too!"

Ryan hung up from his call with Gary enthusiastic and ready to practice. He looked forward to sharing his thoughts with Valerie during their next meeting – on Educator.

Key Ideas from the Influencer Chapter

- Recognizing the power of testimonials
- Sample testimonial letter**
- Show me the money!
- Three Negotiating Tips**
- Using Storytelling

**These tools can be found starting on page 157 and online at www.saleseffectiveness.com/rainmaker

CHAPTER NOTES

_____

_____

_____

_____

_____

_____

_____

"Buyers want to deal with professionals who ask the right questions and truly listen to the answers. They want to work with people who can take what they've heard and translate it into appropriate solutions."

Ken Thoreson

Chapter 9

EDUCATOR

Educator. Ryan thought about the word as he drove to the next meeting with Valerie on Rainmaking. Educating customers seemed pretty simple really... Sales 101. *Know your products and services and make sure you fully explain the features and benefits of your offerings.* He wondered if this would be the key idea of their conversation today.

Arriving at her office, Ryan asked about her vacation; she called it a *'welcome rejuvenation.'* After hearing some of the highlights of her trip, Ryan said, "I'm glad you had a good time – I can't wait for my next vacation. I could use a renewal!"

"I know," said Valerie. "It's very healthy for all of us to take a break. For now, though, are you ready to look into the Educator role?"

"Yes. As I drove over here this morning, I was thinking about this one. In your mind, is the Educator practice mostly around talking with our customers about the features and benefits of our solutions?"

Valerie paused before she responded. "I think there are really two components to the Educator role: Educating the *customer* and educating *yourself*. And both of these components are extremely important to Rainmakers.

"Let's think first about educating customers. We know that *all* salespeople should be intimately knowledgeable about the <u>features</u> of their company and the products and services they sell, right? The *better* salespeople are able to demonstrate to customers how the features of their products and services can provide specific <u>benefits</u> and <u>value</u> to the customer. The *best* go far beyond that."

Ryan said, "Features and benefits have been preached pretty hard to us at Summers. What's that expression? *Features tell. Benefits sell.*"

"Right. And you know I'm always amazed when I hear salespeople stating a product's *features* and thinking the customer automatically connects the benefits and value they will receive. They don't. I can't overstate it – *we must be blatant about tying features to benefits and value for our customers.*"

She continued. "For example, last week on vacation, I wandered in to a bookstore. They happened to be selling a particular brand of e-reader device and I'd been thinking about getting one. Their model cost more than some others so I was trying to compare them. The salesperson that was helping me was very nice and seemed to know her product, but she made comments like *'it has double the battery life of other e-readers.'*

"And I'm thinking, great feature, right? But it's not even on her radar that she needs to provide the benefit – the *'so what'*– to make this feature come alive for me. Now, if she had just added to her statement, *'Think about what this means – you may be at the beach when you're reading… or on a train…or in many places where there's no convenient way to charge your device. Unlike the less expensive model, with our device, you won't have to worry about whether there is a place to charge it – in fact, you can go on a month-long vacation, charging it before you leave, and for the entire month you won't have to even think about whether or not you'll be able to finish reading your book.'*"

"You see what I mean? Now I'm starting to picture what her feature can mean to me… I'm thinking of how upset I'll be when I'm in the middle of a book on a plane and the reader loses its charge. By her painting a picture of the *benefits*, I begin to really get it – and to feel the value that her price represents."

She continued. "And whenever possible, the best salespeople tie the features and benefits to the *dollarized* value the customer will receive. Using my example, assume I am going to use my e-reader for work purposes. What if she began to ask me questions like, *'How much business might you lose if your device won't operate while you're on a two-hour trip with no power?'* After a few questions like that, now I'm beginning to really perceive the *value* – in dollars and cents – that her solution provides."

Ryan sat quietly. He realized – even with the features and benefits training he had gone through – that he didn't always answer the big questions his customers were probably thinking as he talked to them about Summers' solutions: *So what? What's the impact? What's it actually worth? What's in it for me?* He vowed to himself to always consider those questions when talking about solutions with customers.

He said, "A minute ago, you said the *best* salespeople go far beyond features and benefits when working with their customers. What did you mean by that?"

"Just as with the other roles, there are many aspects to the Educator practice beyond the obvious. Let's take a look at the core characteristics of an excellent Educator."

She showed a slide.

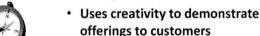

EDUCATOR

- **Product and applications expert**
- **Thought leader**
- **Uses creativity to demonstrate offerings to customers**
- **Coaches and trains – partnering with others**
- **Acts as a source of ideas for customers**
- **Continuous learner**

"We've talked about the fact that an Educator needs to be an *expert* on their products and services. And I mean they know their key products *cold*, including the nuances and distinctions between their offerings and those of their competitors. Even more, they have the ability to make the *application* of their products and services come alive for the customer. They use demonstrations to show specifically how the customer can use the product or service to create value and differentiate themselves."

"I think I'm pretty good in that area," said Ryan. "I really like doing demonstrations for customers and they've told me how much they appreciate my demos."

"Excellent. I've seen many salespeople treat a demo too lightly – they've done it so many times. They forget that for a customer, this could be the first chance – often the only chance – to see it... feel it... experience it. There's a huge value in developing and practicing demonstration skills – even when you've been at it for a while."

Ryan said, "I believe you were the first one I watched doing demos when I began. I've never forgotten the enthusiasm you put into them and your patience with customer questions. It's stuck with me over the years."

Valerie smiled. "That's great to hear. I try to have the mindset that it is a privilege to show someone how we might be able to help them improve their business. It's how I always approach running a demo."

"It shows," said Ryan. "I think that's been one of my strengths as well – and it doesn't hurt that I really believe in our solutions."

"That definitely helps! Now let's talk about how you can go one step further – and that step is to help your customers see you not only as an expert in our products and services, but as a *thought leader* in the industry."

"A thought leader? What do you mean exactly?"
"A thought leader is a person that is recognized by others as someone who deeply understands the business. They fully research the industry, the trends that are occurring, the directions customers are headed, and the entire broad marketplace beyond their own company."

"I feel like all salespeople should be doing that," said Ryan.

"You're right," she replied. "Everyone *should* be doing it to some degree. However, one thing that differentiates a true thought leader from a well-prepared salesperson is that they research far beyond the issues related to the products and services they sell – and they're generous in *sharing* their knowledge with customers."

She continued. "For example, let's say that during your sales calls, you learn that several customers are struggling with security – an issue that your products and services have nothing to do with. Many salespeople would ignore the issue and try to move the conversation back to the needs they *can* address. A thought leader, though, recognizes this as an opportunity – and asks questions about the issue. Later they might spend time researching it in order to put together a list of resources that can help customers address the problem.

"In the future," said Valerie, "when calling on a customer, this salesperson might say, '*During the past year, I've worked with businesses like yours with security* issues. *I've spent time researching the problem and talking to other customers and I compiled this list of resources that have helped many of them. I hope you'll find it useful as well.'* Guess what? The customer sees the salesperson differently when they share that kind of knowledge. It demonstrates not only expertise in the business, but also a commitment to helping them solve problems."

"I like that idea a lot," said Ryan. "Sort of like a Consultant on steroids! Instead of only researching around the customer's business, it's really around the entire industry and their issues."

"Exactly," said Valerie. "Good thought leaders might send customers copies of articles or recommend books with research they've found. I've seen some salespeople even create blogs or interest groups for customers that let them share their ideas and best practices. And typically these salespeople find that by being open with what they learn, their efforts are richly rewarded."

"I believe Carmen may be doing something like that," said Ryan. "I never did get a chance to call her after we talked about the Consultant role a few weeks ago – I really should do that."

"Yes, Carmen is one of the best Educators I know. She's using all kinds of creative ideas to help her customers understand what Summers' solutions can do for them."

"Really? Like what?"

"Why don't you talk with her about it – I'm sure she'll freely share her ideas – she believes in the principle that generosity pays off – with her customers and with her colleagues."

"Thanks, I will." said Ryan.

Valerie continued. "Earlier I said the Educator role had two components – educating the *customer* and educating *yourself*. Let's spend a few minutes on the second component – the idea of self-education."

"Sounds vaguely familiar," laughed Ryan. "You've been talking about continuous learning ever since we began these sessions!"

"I have, haven't I? It could be because this idea is, without question, one of the most important things you can do to become a Rainmaker."

She continued. "I heard a phrase once that has always stuck with me – 'learners are earners.' Have you heard that before?"

"No," said Ryan. "Michelle will get a charge out of that one – she's hoping we can put in a swimming pool next year. If I tell her that quote, she'll push me to read every book out there!"

"Great – sometimes it's helpful to have a little extra motivation!" smiled Valerie. "But the reason that self-learning is so important is simple. To be a source of advice and creative ideas for your customers, you have to cultivate your ability to generate these ideas. How? By making time to educate *yourself*."

Ryan said, "I agree and I understand the value of what you're saying, but I just don't see how I can find more time to do a lot of additional reading."

"Time is always the challenge, isn't it? The good news is, there are many ways you can educate yourself other than reading books. For example, there are thousands of free podcasts you can listen to and many are given by some of the best minds in the country! I listen to them when I'm driving… when I'm on the treadmill … sometimes when I'm making dinner. Use pockets of downtime here and there to do some self-learning. I've found that it's a *mindset* thing and Rainmakers have a relentless thirst for knowledge – the more they learn, the more they *want* to learn."

"What about learning more about how our customers are using our products?" asked Ryan.

"Good question, and one that not enough salespeople ask themselves. A great source of knowledge can come directly from our customers – and you should ask and encourage them to *educate you*… to help you see firsthand the issues people face with our products and services. For example, if you're working with a VP, you might say, *'Joe, would you mind if I spend some time with Matt and Nicole to see how they're using our products?'*"

She continued. "Most customers are happy to oblige – they see it as an opportunity for their people to become 'better' and more efficient. Not only will seeing our products and services in use be a wonderful learning experience for you, it immediately raises your status with the customer. For a big customer, imagine the impact of saying during a business review, '*I spent two days in the field with Matt and Nicole and we found three ways to save time in their process.*' Most customers have never had a salesperson ask to spend time with users, and it's absolutely a win-win."

Ryan thought about his customer base. He could immediately think of two customers where this idea could apply. He remembered back to his earlier conversation with Luis about *bagging more elephants*. This seemed like a perfect technique to use with his larger customers. *And*, he thought, *becoming an expert in how our products and services are applied in the field will give me rich stories to share with current and future customers.*

Valerie said, "The last area I wanted to discuss in the Educator role is the idea of educating yourself on the *personal* side of your customers' lives – their causes, their interests, and sometimes even their family situation. I know you often do this, but it never hurts to remind ourselves of the importance of learning about their interests and better *connecting* with them."

"That is one area where I pride myself," said Ryan. "If a customer has a plaque from an organization they're involved with, I speak about it if it seems appropriate. If they have their college diploma on the wall and I follow that school's football team, I talk about it. I'm very big on identifying with them if I can."

"I'm not surprised – it's that likeability factor again! Connecting can take all kinds of forms. I had one customer whose son had juvenile diabetes and for years I had been participating in the diabetes bike race. This connected us far beyond most customer relationships – we were fighting a common enemy. So learning more about their causes and interests is just one more way of educating *yourself*."

"I like what I've heard today," said Ryan. "And I'm going to try to call Carmen later – to pick her brain a bit. I know she's had some big wins lately."

"Sounds good. So, next time, we'll be talking about the last of the roles – Facilitator. I'm thinking I might invite Luis to join us if you don't mind. With his service background, he's got a terrific perspective on facilitation with customers. But meanwhile, remember, James is coming to town and we're meeting for dinner. You can still come, can't you?"

"I wouldn't miss it," said Ryan. "Shall I pick you up?"

"Let's meet at the restaurant. I have an appointment in the area that afternoon, and I'll just stick around until dinnertime. So, see you soon!"

Later that day...

Carmen responded to Ryan's email request right away. She remembered him from the training session they attended together last year. "I'd love to help!" she wrote back. His email briefly described his discussions with Valerie and he said that Valerie mentioned some creative ideas Carmen was using to educate her customers. They agreed to speak on Sunday evening.

When she called Sunday, Ryan remembered how much he admired Carmen. She was easy to talk to and he could see why customers appreciated her – she laughed easily and made him feel comfortable right away.

"So Valerie called me an Educator, huh? I guess I've been called worse! Okay, so it's true that I'm passionate about sharing information with my customers. And I have a couple of ideas to share with you," said Carmen. "Some things that really helped boost my results."

"Thank you so much," said Ryan. He was gratified at how readily his co-workers were willing to reveal their own sales 'magic.'

Carmen began. "I really feel that the more information I provide my customers about how to improve their business, the more trust I build with them. I even send a monthly tip sheet called 'Carmen Counsels' to many of my customers – it's a bit of a hokie name, I know, but they seem to really like it; I often get several thank you responses each month."

"What's in the tip sheet?" asked Ryan.

"It varies – kind of depends on the mood I'm in! Some months, it's an idea for using our solutions in a different way, and other months it has very little to do with our products and services. It might be an idea I read about – like an innovative way to entertain customers without spending a lot of money or a story that relates to many businesses in their industry. Once a year I even send 'Carmen's favorite clean jokes' that they can tell to any of their customers! I try to make it useful and entertaining so they won't see it as junk mail!"

"And you believe this has really boosted your business?"

"I'm 100% sure of it. In fact, some customers have told me they can't stop doing business with Summers because they'd miss their monthly tip sheet!"

"Wow," said Ryan. "Can you add me to your mailing list? And do you have any other ideas for me?"

"Sure, I'll be happy to send them to you. Another idea you might like started pretty much by accident. Last year, my husband bought me one of those little, hold-in-your-palm video cameras. Do you know the ones I'm talking about?"

"I do. My wife bought us one as well. We haven't used it much yet, though."

"Well, one night I used it to film my son's baseball game. The next day I still had it in my purse when I called on one of my best customers. While I was there, he started telling me how much our solution had helped diminish a problem they'd been facing for several months. I thought to myself, *I wish I had this on tape!* Then I remembered the camera in my bag. I pulled it out and said *'Jerry, would you mind if I asked you to say that again on video?'* He said, *'Sure! I've always wanted to be an actor!'* and we both chuckled and I filmed him talking about how they had successfully used our solution."

She continued. "He gave me permission to show it to others and you wouldn't believe the mileage I've gotten out of that little video clip!"

"Really?" said Ryan. "How so?"

"When I got back to my office, I emailed the clip to two prospects I'd been talking to who were facing similar issues – but they weren't convinced that we could really help them. The next day I had two appointments! And I've used the camera for many other purposes – showing application techniques… unique solutions… things our marketing department can't capture quickly enough to put into our materials. If I'm with a new customer, I pull that little baby out, plug it into my laptop, and – 'it's *show time!*' For the most part, as long as I keep the clips short – less than 3 minutes – customers love it!"

"Great idea," said Ryan. "It reinforces what Valerie shared with me earlier about the power of social proof and testimonials, but this is doing it creatively!"

"Oh, one more thing," said Ryan, thinking back to the Consultant practice. "I remember when you and I were in that training session together and you mentioned creating a meeting agenda with a customer. Is that something you do regularly?"

"Yes. As I said, I'm passionate about communicating with my customers every step of the way. I don't create an agenda for every meeting, but when there are a lot of potential issues at play, I always do. And I often send them a summary after a meeting as well. Doing these things helps my customers view me as a true professional – even though I love to have fun with them!"

"I believe it," said Ryan. Anything else you can share?"
"One last idea that I don't see people taking advantage of in educating customers is to bring in subject matter experts on key calls – to help answer tough questions. I often see salespeople try to handle every issue on their own and honestly, I think that can be very foolish. We have people in Operations or Finance or whatever who are happy to accompany us – if they get some notice. By doing this, the customer sees that there is a whole network of people supporting them. It's a big win."

Carmen paused. "I'm really sorry to have to end this, but my son is getting ready for bed and I want to make sure I tuck him in. I'm glad you're working with Valerie and I'm very intrigued by what you're doing together. I hope this was some help!"

"You have no idea," said Ryan. "Thank you and I hope I can help you in some way in the future. Maybe I'll see you before too long – on the company trip perhaps?"

She laughed, "You'll get there – I feel certain."

Key Ideas from the Educator Chapter

- Articulating the dollarized value
- Being a thought leader
- Learners are earners
- Using video testimonials
- Providing a meeting agenda via e-mail**

**These tools can be found starting on page 157 and online at
www.saleseffectiveness.com/rainmaker

CHAPTER NOTES

_____

_____

_____

_____

_____

_____

_____

"We can do anything we want as long as we stick to it long enough."

Helen Keller

Chapter 10

The Rainmaker Blues...

Leaving each meeting with Valerie, Ryan felt inspired and confident that his career was moving in the right direction. He knew that if he implemented the ideas they discussed within each practice, his progression would accelerate and hopefully he'd move out of 'average.' After their meeting on Educator, his feelings were no different; he even shared some highlights with Michelle the next evening as they went for a walk.

Later that night, however, Ryan couldn't fall asleep – he tossed and turned until he finally crawled out of bed at 3:30 a.m. His brain was wired awake, so he walked into the kitchen, found a pen and paper, and sat down at the table. Soon he began to write notes feverishly.

He didn't realize that Michelle was standing in the doorway a few minutes later until he heard her say, "What's wrong?"

He looked up. "Sorry… I didn't mean to wake you."

"It's okay, but what are you doing in here?"

"I'm not sure. I can't sleep and I feel like my head is swimming. These meetings with Valerie are great and I feel like she's definitely setting me up for success, but right now, I'm overwhelmed. I was just writing a list of the four roles that we've talked about so far – and some of the ideas she shared for each of them. There's so much and I feel like I can't do it all!"

He showed Michelle his notes.

"You see what I mean? And these are just some of the ideas… it doesn't even account for all the things that go into making each one of them actually happen!"

"I see. And I also know that you need to sleep – come on back to bed. Isn't your dinner with Valerie and the guy you called the Hunter – James – tomorrow night? Talk to them about it. As far as I know, every single one of the salespeople at Summers has only 24 hours in a day, just like you. And I'm certain that no one is more capable than you of making the most of every one of those days."

Ryan reluctantly agreed to try and get some sleep. The act of writing the ideas on paper seemed to help somewhat, but he still slept fitfully the rest of the night.

The next evening...

Ryan arrived at the restaurant early – 6:15 – for his 6:30 dinner reservation with Valerie and James. He still felt restless despite completing several good sales calls that day. He waited in the lounge area for Valerie and James. Before long, Valerie walked in, followed within minutes by James, who shook Ryan's hand enthusiastically.

"So you're Valerie's protégé, are you?" said James. "Lucky you – she's one of the best salespeople I ever met! Did she tell you that she sold me on coming to work at Summers last year – and then she left the company?" James chuckled.

"Well that's not exactly how – or why – it happened," smiled Valerie. "But I do have to admit that it made me feel good to know we had you on board before I left – I've still got stock in the company, you know!"

Ryan turned to James. "I've heard a lot of good things about you from Valerie and you're already pretty well known in the ranks – so it's a real pleasure to meet you. Thank you so much for agreeing to have dinner."

"I'm delighted to meet you as well," said James. "Valerie and I spent a little time on the phone talking about what the two of you are working on. I have to say, this is one of the most exciting concepts I've heard in a long time. The idea of trying to specifically identify best practices of top salespeople – within a clear framework of five roles – is very appealing to me."

"To me as well," said Ryan, but he couldn't knock last night's apprehension out of his mind.

Just then, the waiter appeared and took their order. Ryan pushed the nerves out of his head and decided that he'd enjoy the evening, no matter what.

"So James," began Valerie, "as I told you, one of the five roles that we've been exploring is *Hunter*. I shared with Ryan that you are one of the best Hunters I've ever known and that I hope you are willing to share some of your 'secret sauce' as Ryan and I have been calling it."

"I'm flattered," said James. "And I'm happy to share some ideas that have worked well for me. I guess you're right – I'm a Hunter at heart. Winning new business is almost a 'high' for me. So, over the years I've developed some techniques that have definitely helped me feed the fire. Let's start with one thing I've noticed about a lot of salespeople who have good intentions, but never make it to the top."

"What's that?" asked Ryan.

"They don't pay attention to 'time thieves.' The best Hunters are always on the alert for things that steal from their 'selling time'… things like answering email, getting involved in non-customer meetings, planning for future calls, etc. All these things are important and must be done, but I rarely do them between 8 and 2; my own system is to reserve those hours strictly for *selling* so I take care of all of my other work outside those hours. 'Time thieves' get the best of a lot of good salespeople."

Ryan nodded. He remembered Valerie talking about how Rainmakers use a *system* and protect their selling time. He knew he was much more arbitrary about his patterns and how he managed his time. Could setting up a 'system' make that much of a difference?

James continued. "The next area I am very diligent about may be considered passé by some, yet it remains one of the most important ways I know of to help bring in a continuous stream of new business. That's *networking.*"

Ryan said, "Valerie told me when your name first came up that you were one of the best networkers she knows. Can you say more about your techniques?"

"Sure. But first, let me ask you. What do you think of when I say the term 'networking?'"

Ryan thought. "I guess I think of networking as finding opportunities to meet people and sharing what I do in hopes of finding potential new customers."

James nodded. "Okay - I think your view is shared by most salespeople, and frankly, it's too limiting. Let me tell you what *I* mean by networking. Rather than thinking of it as going to functions and handing out my business card to make sure everyone knows what I do, I think of it as building relationships with other people – relationships where I can provide something of value and <u>not</u> expect anything in return."

He paused. "Let me repeat that. I believe networking should involve getting to know people – and them getting to know you – *with no strings attached.* I never approach networking as a way to create sales. The whole goal, in my mind, is to have other people think of me as a valuable resource in *their* network. I am *intentional* in getting to know them – to treat them not as *prospects* but as people I want to learn more about – and to help in whatever way I can."

James continued. "It's really amazing how working hard to develop a reputation of integrity and credibility with people – both inside and outside the industry – builds a network exponentially. Even when people are not involved in our business, if they think of you as a 'good person to know,' they spread your name to others who may be involved in our business."

Valerie asked, "Can you provide some examples of how this has worked for you?"

"Sure. Over the years I've gotten very involved in both local and regional councils in our industry. Outside the business, I've been a Boy's Club volunteer, a member of the advisory board at the YMCA, and a regular volunteer with Habitat, just to name a few. As I get more involved, I meet lots of people and I try to learn as much about them as I can – but *not* with the expectation that they are a potential customer. Over time, we often share stories about our work and I may say something about how I've helped customers with various issues. Sometimes they later share my story with someone else they know. Do you have any idea how many people each person you meet knows?"

Ryan said, "I don't know, maybe 100?"

"For some it's 100 – for others, it could be 250 or even more. So if you think of each person you meet as a potential connection to all the other people in *their* network, you start to see the web that can be built – and every time you make a positive impression with one person, the bands of the web become stronger. I can tell you for a fact that most of my biggest deals have begun in some way through my network."

"No kidding?" said Ryan. "It has that much impact?"

"It can. It might be weeks, months, or even years later but networking is always a solid investment into your future. And again, your motivation should be to help solve problems and add value in whatever you do. This attitude ties very closely to my belief that as a salesperson, my job is to help my customers' improve and grow their business. I'm helping them to change – to become *better.*"

"Would you call yourself a 'catalyst' for change?" asked Valerie.

"That's a great way to put it!" laughed James.

Valerie smiled. "And have you gotten into using some of the social networking web sites to build your network?"

James answered, "Absolutely. The best purpose I have found for these sites is to meet other people that my customers know. This brings me to one of the other ideas that I wanted to talk about tonight – an area that true Hunters make full use of, yet many salespeople ignore."

"What's that?" asked Ryan.

"Referrals. I've read that 70% of salespeople don't ask for referrals because they're uncomfortable doing so. And it's a shame, because referrals are always the best leads you can get and a very important way to build your business. Do you usually ask your customers for referrals?"

Ryan replied, "Occasionally, but I usually don't. I worry that it will put our relationship in an awkward position and I don't want to taint the customer's appreciation for me and for our products and services. I feel like future business could be lost if I turn him or her off that way."

"I think that's what many other salespeople would say as well," said James. "I also think it's an excuse and a poor decision if you want to get to the top. So, let's talk about how I deal with referrals.

"First, because I believe so much in the spirit of reciprocity – *I give, you give, we all win* – I always try to provide my customers with at least one referral to someone *they* may gain value from. And I usually don't wait until the sales cycle is complete to begin asking for referrals. I sometimes joke about it in the middle of the sales process, saying something like, *'Dave, you are really trying to make sure I earn my referrals, aren't you?'* or in a serious vein, *'We are going to do everything possible while working with you to make sure you are confident enough to refer us to others.'*"

He continued. "It's true that some customers are hesitant to provide names of referrals or sometimes they can't even think of names to provide. So I help them. I may say, '*I noticed on LinkedIn that you are connected to Jose Smith at PHS. Do you think you could make an introduction for me?*'

James smiled as he went on. "You may have heard the old sales expression – 'if you don't ASK, you don't GET.' This is equally true about asking for referrals."

Ryan sat quietly. He could see why Valerie defined James as a Rainmaker – and he wondered if he'd ever get there. Valerie's voice interrupted his thoughts.

"Ryan, you're awfully quiet. Anything on your mind?"

He hesitated. Then he decided to take Michelle's advice and tell them what had kept him awake the night before.

He pulled out the notes he had written at the kitchen table and described his sleepless night, ending by saying, "I'm feeling somewhat overwhelmed right now. We've talked about the five roles of a Rainmaker – and each of them has so many good ideas that I should be following. I just don't think I can do it all!"

There was silence for a moment and then Valerie spoke. "I hear what you're saying. And I understand your concerns. It could be pretty overwhelming to think that you need to follow all of these practices with all accounts at *all* stages of the sales process."

She continued. "While most Rainmakers do well in all five of the roles, almost all of them have one or two roles where they especially excel and they place more of their emphasis there. James, for example, is one of the best Hunters I know. It's likely his favorite part of the job. Would you agree, James?"

"Ha! You've nailed me!" said James. "I do love to hunt. But I recognize that there's a lot more to building a stream of ongoing business than hunting for opportunities."

Valerie said, "Just so you'll know, James, we've developed a very straightforward way to view the five roles, and I'd like to get your reaction:

- Hunters *identify* opportunities.
- Consultants, Influencers, and Educators *turn the opportunities into business*.
- And Facilitators *ensure we deliver on our commitments* in order to build customer loyalty.

"Good," said James. "That makes sense to me. What I'd like to add, however, is that I am not as strong in some of the roles as others, so in those areas, I often ask for help from people who are better than me."

"I'm glad you said that," said Valerie. "That was exactly where I was going. Tell us more about that."

"Well, if I have a large opportunity, for example, I might ask someone on our service team to accompany me. I can certainly educate customers on our products, but I look for someone who is better than I am. In response to your concern, Ryan, it's not about *you* doing everything yourself, but it is about giving customers every reason to do business with us. And if that means tapping other people to help you in certain areas, by all means, do it!"

Ryan paused. "I see. So I may not be involved in all the roles for a particular customer. But I may need to be more of an Educator with one, and more of a Facilitator with another. Is that what you're saying?"

"Exactly," said Valerie. "It's a balancing act and what we've been attempting to do is take a look at many of the best ideas from Rainmakers who excel in one or more areas. Hopefully you'll take guidance from all of them and use the ideas when the situation warrants it."

"I appreciate your explanation," said Ryan. "I know I want to be the best salesperson I can be and I was beginning to think I wouldn't make it. I didn't want to give up before I really got going!"

James smiled, "Which leads me to one final tip I have about being a Rainmaker – and particularly a Hunter."

"What's that?" asked Ryan.

"You've got to always maintain two attitudes: **Persistence** and **Resilience**."

"I agree," said Valerie. "Can you say more about those two traits?"

"Yes. Even when you believe in what you're doing – and I very much do – it's not going to be easy to bring in new business. So you absolutely must be persistent. I may ask three or four times for a referral, for example. And I may call on a customer as many as 20 times in some cases before I get any business from them. *That's persistence.*"

He continued. "And let's face reality – in sales, you're going to hear *'No'* a lot. You must let it roll off of you. You may hear *'I'm not interested'* comments 30 times from customers in any given day when you're making phone calls. But you still have to pick yourself up and put the same level of enthusiasm into the 31st call as you did the first. *That's resilience."*

Valerie smiled. "Have either of you ever seen the bracelet that I always wear?"

Both men shook their heads and Valerie pulled up the sleeve of her jacket slightly to reveal a small silver bracelet that was lightly engraved.

"Can you see what it says?" she asked.

"FIDO," said Ryan. "Is that the name of your dog?" He looked puzzled.

"No," said Valerie. "It's not my dog. It stands for *'Forget It. Drive On.'* Sometimes, glancing at this little bracelet has kept me going long after some others have decided *'it's too hard'* or *'I can't handle another rejection.'* And I really believe it. Let things roll off and keep going. It's good for sales…it's good for life."

"You see why she's so well regarded in this industry?" James asked, smiling at Ryan.

"I do," said Ryan. "I've been feeling it all along. Now it's up to me to execute her lessons."

"Strategy equals execution. All the great ideas and visions in the world are worthless if they can't be implemented rapidly and efficiently."

Colin Powell

Chapter 11

FACILITATOR

Ryan left the house early on the morning of his meeting with Valerie on the final Rainmaker practice – *Facilitator*. Since Valerie had invited Luis to join them for this session, they were meeting at The Red Barn for an early breakfast. Driving to the restaurant, Ryan thought about the last several weeks and how much his approach to selling had changed in that time. He knew today's lesson would mean more change, yet it would bring him one step closer to his personal goal of becoming one of the top salespeople in the company.

Pulling in to the parking lot, he found Luis getting out of his car at the same time.

"Hello," said Ryan. "We meet again!"

"Hi Ryan – it's great to see you. When Valerie called me the other day to ask me to join the two of you, I remembered our conversation of a few weeks ago. So how did all of this get started?"

"I was searching for some help and I reached out to Valerie one day. She was interested in developing some research she'd started before leaving Summers and she offered to help me. Did she bring you up to speed on what we're doing?"

"She did. And I must say, I'm impressed. I've done research of my own in the past couple of years and I just don't think there's enough structure provided to a lot of salespeople; most of us need more definition around the many hats we wear. Too often we are given a goal and maybe some basic training and then it's just, 'Go get 'em!' I think defining these five roles makes a lot of sense."

They walked in to the restaurant and spotted Valerie. After greeting each other, they ordered their breakfast and she began.

"So today, we're going to talk about the last of the five Rainmaker roles – the role of Facilitator. I like to say this is where 'the rubber meets the road.' I asked Luis to join us today because in my mind, he is one of the best Facilitators I've ever met."

"Flattery will get you nowhere!" laughed Luis.

"It's true. You provide an excellent model for how a salesperson should deliver a superior customer experience – the hallmark of a good Facilitator."

"Could we back up just a bit?" asked Ryan. "What exactly do you mean by the role of Facilitator?"

"Sorry," said Valerie. "As I've mentioned, the first four roles are the ones that *identify* opportunities and *turn them into business*. A Facilitator makes sure the company *delivers* on its commitments… building customer loyalty and creating superior customer experiences, which will hopefully lead to more business."

She continued. "Just as we've done for the other roles, I've prepared a summary of what makes a strong Facilitator."

FACILITATOR

- **Champions customer needs**
- **Orchestrates resources**
- **Builds internal alliances**
- **Able to put all the pieces together to bring about change**
- **Oversees or leads implementation**
- **Always gives a little bit more**

She turned to Ryan. "So, when would you think most salespeople should put on their Facilitator hat?"

Ryan thought. "I'd say it's after the sale, when the implementation phase begins. Do you agree, Luis?"

"Personally, I'd say that facilitation often begins much earlier. For example, when I create a proposal for a large opportunity I'm working on, I spend a lot of time creating a solid implementation plan to include as part of the proposal. I've been told by more than one customer that my approach to implementation *within the proposal* was the reason they selected our company. They saw that I had thought through the entire process and they believed my plan had the highest chance of execution success. I don't think many of our competitors develop such a thorough plan."

"I would agree," said Valerie, "that it's important to keep your Facilitator hat close by throughout the sales process. It gives your customers confidence that you are a person who delivers on promises."

"That's true," said Luis. "I begin thinking about implementation very early on. It helps ensure that things go smoothly so that in the future my customers *want* to do business with me – they know things will work out as planned."

"That's a frustration I often feel," said Ryan. "No matter how much planning I do, things don't always work out as they should. We miss a delivery or there's a software glitch, or something they've asked for falls through the cracks. Do all of your implementations always work out as planned?"

"Always? No," said Luis. "We'll never achieve 100% accuracy. So, when things go wrong – and things *will* sometimes go wrong – I'm all about superior service recovery."

"Yes," said Valerie. "In fact, one of the things I've been working on this week is a tool that I thought might be helpful for the Facilitator role – it's called *'Top 5 Steps for Service Recovery.* 'Here's what I have so far:"

TOP 5 STEPS FOR SERVICE RECOVERY

1. **RESPOND IMMEDIATELY** – Assume ownership and take action *right away*. The customer notices.
2. **APOLOGIZE** – Sincerely express your regret.
3. **RELATE WITH RESPECT** – Listen intently and demonstrate genuine empathy for the customer's situation.
4. **FIX THE ISSUE** – Ask the customer what they most want to happen and then do everything possible to fix it.
5. **GO THE EXTRA MILE** – Give extra information, follow up in a personal way, or give something that is seen as valuable.

"So," said Valerie, "When issues do arise, the goal is to be on top of them – quickly. You should know about any issues *before* a customer contacts you, and ideally, you've already begun to take corrective steps. A customer may be upset that a mishap occurred, but they'll respect the fact that you're 'on it' if you immediately take action to define and fix the issue."

"Right," said Luis. "I find that I often need to come up with a temporary solution or another alternative, and I always reassure customers that we are working towards a permanent solution. And I let them know that they can contact me any time for updates."

"Just how much of that is my responsibility versus other people in the company?" asked Ryan. "There's no way I can take care of everything."

"Good point," said Valerie. "And that's another reason to introduce the customer to other people within the company early on. While you 'own' the relationship, at times you may need to do a 'handoff' to others to help. If the customer is already familiar with some of the others on the team that will be helping them, it makes the handoff much more successful."

"You know what I do?" said Luis. "If possible, early on I introduce one of our service team members to the customer in person – especially in the case of a large piece of business. If an 'in-person' meeting isn't possible, sometimes I set up a 'virtual meeting' using one of the online meeting tools – where we all can see each other using a webcam and we talk about next steps and future plans. I find that putting a face with a name really helps put the customer at ease."

"That's a great way to help make the handoff run more smoothly," said Valerie.

"However, I never step away completely," said Luis. "I may not check in daily, but it's still *my* customer. I usually check back in at least once a week to make sure the work is progressing. I don't want there to be any surprises on past issues when it's time to look at future opportunities with them. This approach works well; I've had very few customers leave us for a competitor – at least not due to service and implementation issues."

"And those are good ideas even if there are not service issues," said Valerie. "Sometimes you may even need to ask someone else to be the primary person serving the customer in order to free up your time to do more *hunting*. The same principle applies – make sure the customer is well taken care of, but it doesn't have to be *you* that's doing everything. As we've said, we can't be all things to all customers all the time."

"Duly noted," said Ryan, smiling. "Luis, when we talked before, you told me you've been really focusing on building more business with fewer customers. Would you say your Facilitator skills help you with that?"

"Most definitely. One thing I really focus on when I'm working with large opportunities – even though it can be done with any customer – is to act as a *connector*, which I think fits very well into the Facilitator role. Do you know what I'm talking about?"

"I have an idea – but what do you mean exactly?"

"Let's say I hear one of my customers talking about a problem they're experiencing that is related to diversity, which has nothing to do with our products and services, right?"

"Right – I can't think of a correlation."

"But," said Luis, "Because I'm a *connector*, I try to determine if there is anything else I may be able to offer – in terms of a reference – to help them with the issue. Maybe I learn that one of our HR professionals had a similar issue and I think that my customer could benefit from the information. I'll say, *'You know, I believe our HR guy may be able to help your HR guy because we had that problem too. Would you like me to make the introduction?'*

"Guess what? They're going to remember how I helped take away a *pain* that had nothing to do with selling our products and services. Very likely, they will agree to see me again. I try to make connections on all kinds of levels – personal hobbies, medical conditions, opportunities for their business…anything that will help them personally or professionally."

"I do some of that," said Ryan. "But I have to admit I've never made it a focus – it seems to just happen naturally sometimes."

"That's good," said Luis. "I can see that you're the kind of person that likes to help customers in that way. I'll tell you…everyone has things that especially motivate them and if you can determine a customer's motivators and help them 'connect the dots,' you become someone they want to have around."

He continued. "As I said, I've done some research on this topic myself and I found at least seven broad areas that I believe define most people's motivators. For example, let's say 'safety' is a key motivator for one of my customers. This person doesn't like any uncertainty whatsoever. And let's say they're dealing with a project that is very foreign to them so they have lots of anxiety over how it's going to turn out. If I can connect them with someone who can walk them through a similar situation, it supports their need for safety, so the customer really appreciates an introduction like this.

"As a connector," said Luis, "my job is to find out which particular motivator is strongest for a customer – and then try to find ways to support that person through connections. Your goal is to help them have both *personal* wins as well as *professional* wins. "

Valerie sat quietly watching the exchange between Luis and Ryan. She was delighted to see them interact and share ideas. *If only the entire sales force would adopt this attitude,* she thought, *the entire bell-shaped curve could move, bringing more business to the company and more success for all the individuals who made it happen.*

Breakfast was cleared from the table and Luis looked at his watch. "Unfortunately, I have to run – I have an early meeting this morning."

Valerie said, "It's been a wonderful breakfast – a learning breakfast. Thank you so much for joining us and for your willingness to be so open."

"Yes, thank you," said Ryan. "I'm ready to begin using some of your ideas and I really appreciate your help."

"It's been a pleasure. I'd be happy to get together again sometime."

After Luis left, Valerie looked at Ryan.

"So this was the last meeting we had planned. How do you feel about that?"

"I feel sort of like the kid who knows how to swim, but now he wants to be one of the best on the team. So the coach spends extra time with him, giving him private lessons and the other top swimmers also spend time with him teaching him their best techniques so that he can reach his goal. I fully recognize that this isn't something you or the others had to do, but you were all willing to help me and I will be forever grateful. Thank you."

"You're welcome. Becoming a Rainmaker is not a solitary journey; in my mind, selling is all about *collaboration*. You may not have fully realized it, but during these past few weeks, I've been encouraging you to reach out to others, to collaborate, to learn from each other. Even though in sales we're sometimes 'lone wolves,' the best Rainmakers and sales catalysts see themselves as part of a team."

She continued. "We've covered a lot of ground in the past few weeks. It's difficult to summarize all we've done, but I'd like you to take away a few key points as we conclude our time together:

- First, embrace the role of being a Sales *Catalyst* fully. You *are* a change agent, with your primary mission being to help individuals and organizations improve their businesses. As a change agent, you must believe in the value you bring to your customer. They sense your beliefs and they will act on them.

- Look at the five Rainmaker roles as 'mental models' to strive toward. Models help us remember things and give us something to hold up as a guide. People who use models build skill mastery and 'get there' faster. Work to excel in one or two of the roles, and continually seek to improve in the others.

- And finally, continue to seek feedback from others. Build your network of Hunter coaches, Consultant coaches, etc. Rainmakers surround themselves with other successful people — they know they can't do it alone and make sure *you* coach others whenever they approach you seeking help."

Ryan nodded and picked up the check from the table. "I'll make every effort to do all of those things." He paused. "Again, thank you *so* much."

Valerie smiled. "I've enjoyed it as well ... and it's really helped me clarify the five roles. And, on that note, I have a terrific piece of news to share with you!"

"What's that?"

"I've been talking to Bob Nichols, our sales VP, for the past couple of weeks. The company has decided to fully embrace the initiatives recommended by the Sales Excellence Council and Bob has asked me to head up the council! I've talked to him about the five roles and they resonated really well with him as well. We think this framework will establish the charter for the initiatives that will be implemented; over the next year or so we'll be rolling it out to the entire sales team."

"Wow," said Ryan. "So we might see more of each other after all – congratulations! I guess I've gotten a jump start on the rest of the sales organization."

"You definitely have. And we may actually be working together. I plan to ask a few sales pros from various regions to be part of the council and I'd like to invite you to join us."

"That would be tremendous – thank you!"

An hour later...

Michelle was washing dishes when Ryan walked into the house after his last meeting with Valerie, obviously in good spirits and motivated.

"You look inspired!" she said. "I guess the last meeting was a success?"

"It was – and now Valerie is actually coming back to the company to head up our Sales Excellence Council. And, get this... she's asked me to be part of it!"

"No kidding! I tell you Ryan, I can't believe what a positive perspective you've developed in the past few weeks - you seem so upbeat!"

"For the first time in a long while, I feel upbeat. It's amazing what having a model and a fresh set of insights can do for your outlook."

"You should be really proud of yourself for sticking your neck out and asking for help. I know it wasn't easy at first, but aren't you glad you did?"

"Glad doesn't begin to describe it. I'm going to be the poster boy for 'continuous improvement' from now on – and for reaching out to others for help. And thank you for all you did to challenge me to reach out and connect with Valerie. I'm not sure I would have done it without your encouragement."

Michelle laughed. "I've known all along that you have big potential – I think we're in for lots of rain!"

Key Ideas from the Facilitator Chapter

- Having an implementation plan
- Awareness of the seven motivators**
- Top five steps for service recovery**
- Components of a sales proposal**
- Being a 'connector'

**These tools can be found starting on page 157 and online at www.saleseffectiveness.com/rainmaker

CHAPTER NOTES

_____
_____
_____
_____
_____
_____

"It's nice to believe that if you find the field where you're naturally gifted, you'll be great from day one, but it doesn't happen. There's no evidence of high-level performance without experience or practice.

You will achieve greatness only through an enormous amount of hard work over many years. The best people in any field are those who devote the most hours to what the researchers call 'deliberate practice.'"

Geoffrey Colvin

Authors' Comments

"Ah," said Valerie. "It sounds to me like you want to become a *Rainmaker.*"

For the many years we have been in the sales profession, there has always been curiosity and wonder around how one becomes a 'Rainmaker.' Salespeople recognize the impact that *making rain* could have on their careers and thousands have asked us what it takes to outperform others and be recognized as one of the most consistent producers in their industry. While many articles and books highlight the characteristics of top producers, we hope that our research, as depicted through the ideas in this story, provides a framework that encourages you to pursue excellence and mastery in the sales profession.

Everyone has the potential to become a Rainmaker. But *not* everyone has the drive, determination and commitment to deliberate practice that it takes to be seen as a 'difference-maker' to their customers. If becoming a Rainmaker is your goal, by following the guidelines developed in this book you can pursue the habits of great sales professionals, and in so doing, create *lift* for yourself and your organization. We believe that *making rain*, above anything else, is an attitude… a disposition towards professional excellence…a commitment to help and provide value in every customer interaction.

One of the best things about the sales profession is that few environments can provide the sense of autonomy and freedom that those in this profession enjoy. Yet, the days of primarily focusing on building personal relationships as the core skill of selling are gone. As important as relationships are, tomorrow's sales pro requires a set of interdependent skills that demand continuous enhancement to make a difference. Those skills, integrated into the roles of Hunter, Consultant, Influencer, Educator, and Facilitator, will help transform you into one of tomorrow's sales leaders.

We wish you the best in your journey and we hope that the ideas and tools provided here and on our website will be useful as you pursue your own path towards sales excellence.

Carlos Quintero
Nancy Sutherland

TOOLS AND RESOURCES

Some of the tools referred to in this book appear on the following pages. These tools and other resources can also be downloaded at our website at:
www.saleseffectiveness.com/rainmaker

HUNTER:
- ABCD opportunity grid
- White Spaces key players worksheet

CONSULTANT:
- Fishbone analysis
- List of powerful questions

INFLUENCER:
- Sample testimonial letter
- Negotiation tips

EDUCATOR:
- Sample customer meeting agenda e-mail

FACILITATOR:
- The seven motivators
- Top five steps for service recovery
- Key components of a sales proposal

Submit Your Tools!
We encourage you to send us any tools you have found useful in your selling efforts. E-mail info@saleseffectiveness.com.
If chosen, we will send you a free CD of our book, *Catalyst⁵- Making the Leap from Sales Manager to Sales LEADER!*

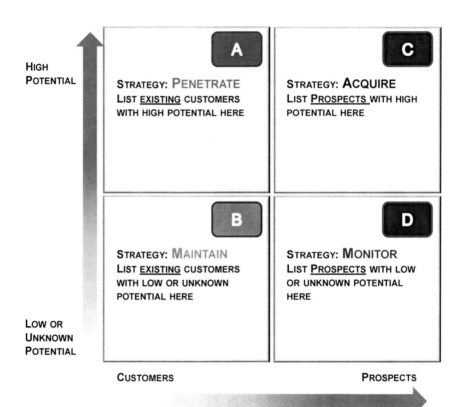

ABCD OPPORTUNITY GRID

HIGH
POTENTIAL

A

STRATEGY: PENETRATE
LIST <u>EXISTING</u> CUSTOMERS
WITH HIGH POTENTIAL HERE

C

STRATEGY: ACQUIRE
LIST <u>PROSPECTS</u> WITH HIGH
POTENTIAL HERE

B

STRATEGY: MAINTAIN
LIST <u>EXISTING</u> CUSTOMERS
WITH LOW OR UNKNOWN
POTENTIAL HERE

D

STRATEGY: MONITOR
LIST <u>PROSPECTS</u> WITH LOW
OR UNKNOWN POTENTIAL
HERE

LOW OR
UNKNOWN
POTENTIAL

CUSTOMERS   PROSPECTS

WHITE SPACES KEY PLAYERS WORKSHEET

Create a worksheet similar to the one below. On it, write the names of the people in the customer's organization that are in the 'white spaces' of the organization chart. These reflect the people you should get to know since they may be important influencers in the sales process. Specify their position in the organization and indicate whether you have met them or not. State what you believe to be their interest, concerns or motivators.

NAME	POSITION	MET?	INTERESTS, CONCERNS, MOTIVATORS

FISHBONE ANALYSIS

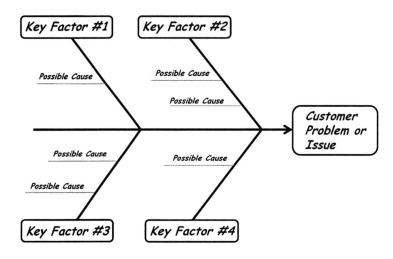

1. Draw a horizontal line (the backbone) in the center of the page.

2. In the fish "head" (the box on the right side of the diagram) write the problem statement (or what is occurring now). Include as much information as possible, including the what, where, when and how much as related to the problem.

3. Draw and label 4-6 "spines" – the key factors or major categories that could be contributing to the problem. Sample categories that are often used as key factors include things like:

People	Marketing	Suppliers
Procedures	Competition	Systems
Product	Service	Price
Materials	Management	Policies

4. Now, brainstorm for causes that may be contributing to the problem. Place these ideas as "cause bones" tied to the appropriate key factor.

5. Select the most likely causes and then investigate each one further to determine the root cause(s) of the issue or problem.

LIST OF POWERFUL QUESTIONS

1. How do you see your business growing in the next several years?
2. What are your objectives from a profitability perspective?
3. What has changed most about your business in the last year?
4. What is the value that you offer your customers?
5. What costs / targets have you established for this project?
6. What do your customers most value your company for
7. What goals have you established for yourself?
8. What is keeping you from achieving them?
9. What problems have you been experiencing?
10. When this occurs, what are the results?
11. Why is the problem occurring?
12. What are the biggest challenges you are facing?
13. What criteria will you use to select who you will work with?
14. What differentiates your business against competitors?
15. What is the competition doing that you should be doing?
16. What has prevented you from doing that?
17. What are your plans to outdistance your competition?
18. Please share more about your staff and how you are organized.
19. What is the worst-case scenario, if you are unable to _____?
20. Can you put a number to that?
21. On a scale of 1-10 how satisfied are you with _____?
22. What is the positive / negative impact on the bottom line?
23. What payback will you receive if this works?
24. What are the consequences, both positive and negative of these trends?
25. What is this costing you in resources and dollars?
26. What financial benefits would you realize if you could _____?
27. What conditions need to be satisfied for our companies to do business together?
28. What level of service do you expect?
29. What factors are important to you in moving forward?
30. If you choose our company to do business with, what results will you expect?

SAMPLE TESTIMONIAL LETTER

Date:

During the past year, we have worked with Summers Inc. and specifically with Valerie Monroe to establish a more efficient process model for our Operations division. We evaluated many companies prior to making a buying decision; our choice to go with Summers was largely based on Valerie's thorough and professional evaluation of our current issues and our confidence in her ability to see us through the entire change process. She established credibility with our entire team and her assessment of the value that her solutions would provide was spot on.

In addition to understanding the issues that were driving our need for change, Valerie helped us anticipate the potential outcomes of our decisions. We estimate a 300% return on our investment to date and the benefits continue as our market share increases.

Valerie challenged our thinking in a very tactful and diplomatic way and she helped us develop a strategy that has paid huge dividends not only for our division and our company but also for our customers.

Valerie and Summers have my highest endorsement.

NEGOTIATION TIPS

TIP # 1 – BUY TIME

When you reach an impasse with a customer, the first strategy is to buy some time. Don't react right away. Ask the customer for a day or two if possible to reflect on the situation and allow you to consider alternatives.

TIP # 2 – SEE THINGS FROM THE CUSTOMER'S PERSPECTIVE

The second tip is to see things from their perspective. You don't have to agree with them, but you can acknowledge their position. This lets them know that you are listening to them and that you are willing to explore options and interests with them.

TIP # 3 – REFRAME

The third tip is to change the situation a bit. Consider changing the timing of the deal, for example, or the terms and conditions, or the way both you and the customer think about the situation. In all cases when you reframe, use the word "we" to connote that you are in this together. This tip is sometimes hard to do but it can be powerful.

SAMPLE CUSTOMER MEETING AGENDA E-MAIL

John,

Thank you again for your willingness to meet on _____.
I look forward to seeing you at 9 a.m.

In reflecting on this first meeting, I have prepared a few questions I would like for us to consider. These questions can serve as our agenda of sorts. Your answers to these questions and others will provide us with a stronger sense of your direction and define how we may potentially be a resource to you.

Have a good week!

1. _____ is known for its leadership in the _____ industry. As you continue to seek areas for growth, what is your short and long-term strategic vision and plans?

2. In light of this direction, how will your organization have to change in the near future?

3. What strategies have worked well in the past? Why?

4. What strategies have NOT worked well in the past? Why?

5. What are the biggest hurdles your people face in working with their customers?

6. If cost and resources were not a constraint, what would you like to achieve as a result of our involvement with your company?

THE SEVEN MOTIVATORS

The following are brief definitions of the seven motivators that drive behaviors. You should recognize and align to them when working with customers as they often influence their buying decisions: Most people are motivated by one or more of the following:

- **BELONGING.** A need to be seen as "fitting in" within the organization.

- **ADVANCEMENT.** A desire to be promoted to a higher position in the organization.

- **RECOGNITION.** A need to be formally acknowledged for contributions.

- **SAFETY.** A desire to avert problems, issues and conflict.

- **ORGANIZATION.** A need for order and structure in the workplace.

- **ACHIEVEMENT.** A strong desire to attain and accomplish tasks or goals.

- **POWER.** A need for authority and strong influence over others in the workplace.

TOP FIVE STEPS FOR SERVICE RECOVERY

1. **RESPOND IMMEDIATELY** – Assume ownership and take action *right away*. The customer notices.

2. **APOLOGIZE** – Sincerely express your regret.

3. **RELATE WITH RESPECT** – Listen intently and demonstrate genuine empathy for the customer's situation.

4. **FIX THE ISSUE** – Ask the customer what they most want to happen and then do everything possible to fix it.

5. **GO THE EXTRA MILE** – Give extra information, follow up in a personal way, or give something that is seen as valuable.

KEY COMPONENTS OF A SALES PROPOSAL

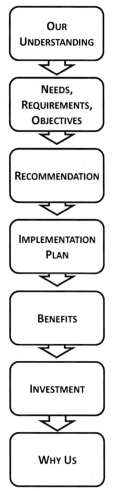

OUR UNDERSTANDING

Summarize your understanding of the customer's situation, including what is happening currently, what problems or challenges they are experiencing, and other key issues.

NEEDS, REQUIREMENTS, OBJECTIVES

This section recaps your understanding of the customer's specific needs, requirements and the objectives they have for the solutions you offer.

RECOMMENDATION

Here you highlight the specific details of your solution, the rationale for each component and the call to action you wish the customer to take.

IMPLEMENTATION PLAN

A table highlighting how your solution will be implemented, including time lines, and who is responsible for each step of the implementation. This should also indicate where you need the customer's involvement.

BENEFITS

A summary of how the customer will specifically benefit as a result of using your solution. Specifically highlight the financial and non-financial value that will occur as a result of moving forward.

INVESTMENT

Recap of the financial investment that will be incurred. Here you will also highlight your organization's terms and conditions, and other payment requirements.

WHY US

This section describes the key benefits of working with your company – including profiles of key people that the customer may work with, and testimonials and other awards you and your company have received that may be relevant for this customer.

Bibliography

Quintero, Carlos and Sutherland, Nancy. *Catalyst[5] – Making the Leap from Sales Manager to Sales LEADER.* Sales Effectiveness, Inc., 2009

Pink, Daniel. *A Whole New Mind.* Riverhead Books, 2005.

Goleman, Daniel. *Emotional Intelligence.* Bantam, 2006

Fox, Jeffrey. *How to be a Rainmaker.* Hyperion, 2000

Cialdini, Robert. *Influence.* Harper Paperbacks, 2006

Stevens, Howard. *Achieve Sales Excellence.* Platinum Press, 2006

Sales Effectiveness, Inc. primary and secondary research.

Sales Effectiveness
INCORPORATED

Sales Effectiveness, Inc. focuses solely on helping Senior Executives drive excellence and accelerate growth for their sales forces. Since 1997, Sales Effectiveness, Inc. has become famous for helping our customers build high performance sales teams.

We believe that in order to improve sales performance, leaders must:

- *Hire correctly* to build a superior team.
- *Plan effectively* in order to drive execution.
- *Develop skills mastery* in order to grow capability.
- *Build Sales Manager excellence* in order to make raising-the-bar a *way of life.*
- *Reward and recognize* continuously in order to drive results.

At SEI, we value each of our customers and we make every effort to model the skills and behaviors Valerie, Ryan and all their peers bring to life throughout this book.

Our team is dedicated to raising the bar for sales professionals worldwide. All the associates of Sales Effectiveness are students of sales and believe that sales excellence is within the reach of all sales teams – with the right leadership, focused education, and a sustained commitment to continuous improvement.

For further information, go to
www.saleseffectiveness.com
or call 770-552-6612

About the Authors

Carlos Quintero is the founder of Sales Effectiveness Inc., a sales excellence consulting and performance improvement firm based in Atlanta, GA. Carlos has 'carried the bag,' led sales teams, and has held highly successful assignments with Procter & Gamble, ARAMARK, Learning International, and Mercer Consulting.

Carlos is passionate about the sales profession and helps companies build a culture of sales excellence and continuous improvement. Customers recognize him as an energetic advisor and mentor with a wealth of knowledge and experience in implementing new ideas.

Carlos is also the author of *Building a World Class Selling Organization*, a framework for sales excellence for business-to-business selling teams. You can reach Carlos at carlos@saleseffectiveness.com.

Nancy Sutherland is a writer and instructional designer with Sales Effectiveness Inc. She is able to take conceptual ideas and make them come to life, as evidenced by the easygoing story format of this book, which, as with all her writing, people find straightforward and insightful.

Nancy's engaging demeanor and listening skills enable her to immediately connect with people and to extract the true story. Her ability to translate ideas into meaningful business communications allows her work to be easily understood and adapted to one's own business. You can reach Nancy at nancy@saleseffectiveness.com.

Carlos and Nancy are also the authors of *Catalyst⁵ – Making the Leap from Sales Manager to Sales LEADER*.

Quick Order Form

To order additional copies of this book:

☎ **Phone orders**: Call 770-552-6612. Have your credit card ready.

⌨ **Online orders**: www.saleseffectiveness.com

✉ **Mail orders:**
> Sales Effectiveness, Inc.
> 570 W. Crossville Rd. Suite 103
> Roswell, GA 30075

Please send _____ copies of *RAINMAKER! Making the Leap from Salesperson to Sales CATALYST.*

Name:		
Address:		
City:	State:	Zip:
Telephone:		
e-mail:		

Price: $15.95 per book.

Shipping: Add $4 for the first book and $1 for each additional book being shipped to the same address (within the U.S.)

Please make checks payable to "Sales Effectiveness, Inc."

◆ **Sales Effectiveness**
I N C O R P O R A T E D

CPSIA information can be obtained at www.ICGtesting.com
Printed in the USA
241929LV00002B/3/P

9 780967 625546